THE ARABS

THE ARABS

THE ARABS

**Other books in the
Coming to America series:**

THE ARABS

Joan Brodsky Schur, *Book Editor*

Bruce Glassman, *Vice President*
Bonnie Szumski, *Publisher*
Helen Cothran, *Managing Editor*
Laura K. Egendorf, *Series Editor*

GREENHAVEN PRESS
An imprint of Thomson Gale, a part of The Thomson Corporation

THOMSON
™
GALE

Detroit • New York • San Francisco • San Diego • New Haven, Conn.
Waterville, Maine • London • Munich

LIBRARY OF CONGRESS CATALOGING-IN-PUBLICATION DATA

The Arabs / Joan Brodsky Schur, book editor.
    p. cm. — (Coming to America)
Includes bibliographical references and index.
ISBN 0-7377-2148-0 (lib. : alk. paper)
    1. Arab Americans—History. 2. Arab Americans—Biography. 3. Arabs—United States—History. I. Schur, Joan Brodsky. II. Coming to America (San Diego, Calif.)
E184.A65.A718 2005
973'.04927—dc22   2004052356

Printed in the United States of America

CONTENTS

Chapter 2: Adapting Old Ways to a New World

Chapter 3: A Marginalized Minority

Chapter 4: Arab Americans of Distinction

FOREWORD

In her popular novels, such as *The Joy Luck Club* and *The Bonesetter's Daughter*, Chinese American author Amy Tan explores the complicated cultural and social differences between Chinese-born mothers and their American-born daughters. For example, the mothers eat foods and hold religious beliefs that their daughters either abhor or abstain from, while the daughters pursue educational and career opportunities that were not available to the previous generation. Generation gaps occur in almost all families, but as Tan's writings show, such differences are even more pronounced when parents grow up in a different country. When immigrants come to the United States, their initial goal is often to start a new life that is an improvement from the life they experienced in their homeland. However, while these newcomers may intend to fully adapt to American culture, they inevitably bring native customs with them. Immigrants have helped make America broader culturally by introducing new religions, languages, foods, and different ways of looking at the world. Their children and subsequent generations, however, often seek to cast aside these traditions and instead more fully absorb mainstream American mores.

As Tan's writings suggest, the dissimilarities between immigrants and their children are manifested in several ways. Adults who come to the United States and do not learn English turn to their children, educated in the American school system, to serve as interpreters and translators. Children, seeing what their American-born schoolmates eat, reject the foods of their native land. Religion is another area where the generation gap is particularly pronounced. For example, the liturgy of Syrian Christian services had to be translated into English when most young Syrian Americans no longer knew how to speak Syriac. Numerous Jews, freed from the European ghettos they had lived in, wished to assimilate more fully into the surrounding culture and began to loosen the traditional dietary and ritual requirements under which they had grown up. Reformed Judaism, which began in Germany, thus found a strong foothold among young Jews born in America.

However, no generational experiences have been as significant as that between immigrant mothers and their daughters. Living in the United States has afforded girls and young women opportunities they likely would not have had in their homelands. The daughters of immigrants, in some cases, live entirely different lives than their mothers did in their native nations. Where an Arab mother may have only received a limited education, her American-raised daughter enjoys a full course of American public schooling, often continuing on to college and careers. A woman raised in India might have been placed in an arranged marriage, while her daughter will have the opportunity to date and choose a husband. Admittedly, not all families have been willing to give their daughters all these new freedoms, but these American-born girls are frequently more willing to declare their wishes.

The generation gap is only one aspect of the immigrant experience in the United States. Understanding immigrants' unique and shared experiences and their contributions to American life is an interesting way to study the many people who make up the American citizenry. Greenhaven Press's Coming to America series helps readers learn why more people have moved to the United States than to any other nation. Selections on the lives of immigrants once they have reached America, from their struggles to find employment to their experiences with discrimination and prejudice, help give students insights into stereotypes and cultural mores that continue to this day. Finally, profiles of prominent immigrants help the reader become aware of the many achievements of these people in fields ranging from science to politics to sports.

Each volume in the Coming to America series takes an extensive look into a particular immigrant population. The carefully selected primary and secondary sources provide both historical perspectives and firsthand insights into the immigrant experience. Combined with an in-depth introduction and a comprehensive chronology and bibliography, every book in the series is a valuable addition to the study of American history. With immigrants comprising nearly 12 percent of the U.S. population, and their children and grandchildren constantly adding to the population, the immigrant experience continues to evolve. Coming to America is consequently a beneficial tool for not only understanding America's past but also its future.

INTRODUCTION

Americans of Arab descent have been part of the American mosaic for over a century. Over 3 million Americans trace their ancestry to an Arab country. However, until recently, few Americans took much interest in knowing about their Arab American neighbors—when and why their families came to America, what obstacles they faced assimilating, and what contributions they made to American life. Only after the terrorist attacks of September 11, 2001, which were perpetrated by nineteen terrorists from Arab countries, did most Americans begin to wonder about the history of Arabs in America.

The September 11 attacks were committed by Arab Muslims who claimed to be following the dictates of Islam, yet immediately afterward Muslims around the world condemned the attacks as un-Islamic. This situation prompted many Americans to realize how little they knew about Islam, the world's second-largest religion. Thus it comes as no surprise that Americans are keenly interested in learning about the faiths of Arab Americans.

In the United States misconceptions about Arabs and Muslims abound. Few Americans realize, for example, that Arabs constitute only around 20 percent of Muslims worldwide, and still fewer know that most Arab Americans practice Christianity. True, many Christian Arabs adhere to religious practices that are sometimes unfamiliar to Americans. This is because most belong to a variety of Eastern Christian sects (known as rites) which include the Orthodox Antiochian, Syrian, Greek, and Coptic churches, and Catholic sects such as the Maronites and Melchites. The history of these churches is significantly different from that of Western Christianity, including Roman Catholicism and Protestantism, with which most Americans are familiar.

When Christian and Muslim Arab immigrants came to America, they brought with them a strong identity based on their religious affiliations and a determination to transplant their faiths to their new home. The prejudice they encountered in America included pressure to abandon their faiths or to change them so that they would conform to American mores. As a result, Arab religious practices underwent some change as the immigrants adapted to a new environment, but Arab Americans also impacted U.S. faiths. Indeed, they have succeeded in diversifying the religious landscape of America, beginning in the first quarter of the twentieth century.

Arab Christians Leave Their Homelands

Historians estimate that more than one hundred thousand Arabs left their homelands for America by 1914. Of this first wave of Arab immigrants, 90 percent were Christian. They came from the Ottoman Province of Greater Syria, a region that included present-day Jordan, Lebanon, Syria, and Israel and the occupied Palestinian territories. This part of the Ottoman Empire, which was ruled by the Turks, included the region where three monotheistic faiths first took root. While Muslims comprised the vast majority of the population in the Ottoman Empire, the Turks protected minority religions under the millet system, whereby each sect became essentially self-governing.

Although Christians were a minority in Greater Syria, the main reason they left their homeland was not to escape religious persecution but to better their economic prospects. Parts of Greater Syria were overpopulated, others too arid to farm. Historian Alixa Naff writes, "Despite the cultivation of virtually every available inch of suitable land and the prevalence of family gardens and private orchards, [the] Mount Lebanon [region of Greater Syria] was unable to produce enough to feed its population."[1] In addition, competition from European industries was making the handicrafts of the region obsolete. The silk industry on which many Arabs depended was in the doldrums, affected by a silk worm blight and competition from elsewhere. By the late nineteenth century Ottoman rule was inept at best and oppressive at worst.

The dream of a better life in America was planted in part by the American Protestant missionaries who had come to the Middle East in the mid–nineteenth century to convert Muslims. While they did not succeed in Christianizing Muslims, they built modern hospitals and schools, which inspired Christian Arabs to dream of a better life in America. (Muslims desiring a better life were more likely to leave for Egypt or another Muslim country rather than risk the unknown in a Christian country that might not welcome them.)

Arab Christians in America

This first generation of Arab immigrants put down roots in New York City, where they learned the peddling trade. Arab pack peddlers sold everything from sewing needles, buttons, and thread, to fancy bed linens and exotic silks. Capitalizing on their origins in the Middle East, they also sold holy water and rosaries that they claimed were imported from the Holy Land but which were in fact made in America. As they plied their wares throughout America, Arab immigrants gradually dispersed throughout the country, settling in relatively small numbers in many communities.

The Syrians, as this first generation was then called, were further subdivided into the various sects of Eastern

Christianity. This division made it difficult for the members of any one sect to establish a large enough community to build a church and hire a priest. Despite these challenges, by 1920 seventy-five Eastern churches were established throughout twenty-eight states.

Unfamiliar with Eastern churches, many Americans assumed that they were backward or inferior to Western churches. Sociologist Philip M. Kayal writes, "Eastern rites were looked down upon socially, being associated with peasant culture, whereas Latin rite [Roman Catholicism] stood for European and Christian civilization, progress, prestige, education and commerce."[2] Practitioners of Eastern faiths therefore came under pressure to convert or modify their traditions if they wanted to move up the social ladder in America. Most susceptible were Arab Catholic sects like the Maronites and Melchites, which came under pressure from America's Roman Catholic hierarchy to follow the dictates of the pope. These groups made various accommodations, for example, by abandoning the ordination of married clergy, insisting instead that their priests remain celibate.

The ways in which the Syrian Orthodox adapted to America illustrates the types of accommodations made by many other Eastern sects of Christianity as well. One eventual change was that men and women, who sat in separate sections in church in their homelands, worshipped side by side in America. Another change was the addition of a choir to services. In addition, over time many American-born offspring could no longer understand the languages of their homelands and so the liturgy was translated into English. According to Middle East expert Joseph Schechla, "Translating the liturgy into the vernacular helped to integrate new immigrants into the English-speaking environment and encouraged the participation of the second American-born generation in the church."[3] The Syrian Orthodox in America also changed their calendar from the traditional Julian to the Gregorian calendar, which was adopted in the sixteenth century by Western Christianity. This enabled them to celebrate holidays like Christmas with their fellow Americans.

Like all members of Eastern Christian traditions, the Syrian Orthodox lost many members when they married out of the faith—one route to assimilation in America. But they retained almost twice as many members as they lost and by the 1980s numbered seventy-five thousand affiliated members. They have grown as they have welcomed the Orthodox of other ethnic groups (such as the Greeks and Russians) into their churches. Thus they maintained their faith while adapting to America, and as a result, increased and diversified the variety of Christian traditions practiced in the United States.

Arab Muslims in America

In contrast to Arab Christians, who were at least somewhat familiar to Christian Americans, Muslims observed an alien religion and were therefore often viewed with mistrust. Islam was virtually unknown in America until Arab Muslims settled in the United States during the first wave of immigration. Although most Arab immigrants are Sunni, followers of other Muslim sects such as the Shiites, Alewites, and Druze (an offshoot of Islam) have arrived as well. The first Muslims to leave Arab countries did so for the same reasons that their Christian neighbors did, but the venture seemed riskier; Muslims left behind their majority status in the Arab world for a country ignorant of their religion.

Once in America, Muslim men were less likely than Christian Arabs to become peddlers. Arriving in force nearly a decade after the first Christian Arabs, the peddling business was already being supplanted by the growth of retail stores. Also, many Muslim men felt uncomfortable entering the homes of strange women because Islamic traditions discourage the intermingling of men and women who are not family members. It was more common for Muslim men to become small shop owners. This way they could keep their family intact: Family members who lived above the store could help out with the business. Muslim men were also drawn to work in the growing auto industry in Detroit, where they could work among other men, many of whom were also Muslim. As word reached the homelands that Muslims could attain success in America, especially in the auto industry, increased migration followed. Today the greater Detroit area has the highest concentration of Arab Americans living in the United States. Like their fellow Arabs who were Christian, Arab Muslims also spread widely throughout the states, settling near factory towns in Ohio and Illinois, for example, and forming sizable communities in California.

In many ways Islam was an easy religion to transport. For Muslims any clean place free of distraction can become a space for prayer. Worshippers have a direct relationship with God, and the intermediary functions of a priest are not required for prayer. In America the first communal prayers were held in homes, with the most knowledgeable man acting as prayer leader. The first community to build a mosque did so in Ross, North Dakota, in 1920. However, according to sociologist Sharon McIrvin Abu-Laban, "These Pioneer Muslims lived in isolation from newcomers and supportive institutions. Over time they lost the use of their native Arabic, 'Christianized' their names, and intermarried."[4] Their lack of success at transplanting their religion was not due to persecution but rather to their small numbers and lack of Islamic institutions.

As the pioneering generation of Muslim Arabs prospered economically in their new homeland, they inspired other members of their extended families to immigrate as well. With a growing population it became easier to maintain their faith. Between 1919 and 1922, two Islamic associations were established in the Detroit area. In 1925 the residents of Michigan City, Iowa, established a mosque that is still in use today. In 1934 a mosque and Islamic center were dedicated in Cedar Rapids, Iowa.

Over time Muslim Arabs, like their Christian counterparts, found that they needed to adapt their religious practices to American lifestyles. In their homelands religious leaders and scholars called imams helped Muslims interpret the ways in which Islamic law, or sharia, applies to daily life. Not only were trained imams in short supply in the United States, but it was often difficult to follow their guidance in a new land. Practicing Muslims found it impossible to pray five times a day unless they were self-employed. Schools and employers did not provide halal meats (from animals that are slaughtered according to Islamic law by methods that minimize suffering), nor did employers make accommodations for those Muslims who fasted from sunrise to sunset during the Muslim month of Ramadan. These impediments made it difficult for devout

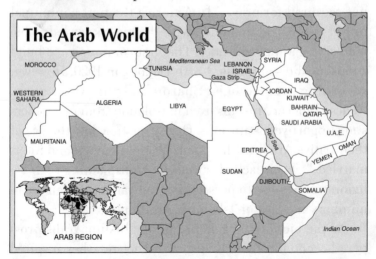

Muslims to fulfil their religious duties, and Muslims began to adapt their faith to life in America. For example, Friday prayers called *jumah* (congregational noontime worship) in the Muslim world, were switched to Sundays in America to ensure that the community had one day on which it could worship together.

Increasingly the mosque took on functions it did not have in the Middle East. For one, it became a place where both sexes could gather for social occasions. According to historian Yvonne Yazbeck Haddad, "Like churches . . . [some mosques in America] often hold bake sales to raise money and potluck suppers as social occasions for their members. Events in these mosques have made it possible for families to socialize with each other."[5] Muslim women, who have traditionally had a much smaller role in the mosque than men, have taken on important roles in raising funds to build mosques, and they teach in Islamic "Sunday schools." At the Islamic Center of Southern California, women have routinely served as board members.

Conflicts Between the First and Second Waves of Muslim Arab Immigration

The second wave of Arab immigration, which began after World War II, was 60 percent Muslim. Between 1965 and 1992 it is estimated that more than four hundred thousand Arab immigrants came to America. Among these newcomers were many educated professionals such as engineers, doctors, and scientists. They arrived from a variety of countries and included Palestinians, Jordanians, Egyptians, Lebanese, Yemenis, and Iraqis. While many were secularists, increasing numbers of devout Muslims arrived in the 1970s, including university students.

These newcomers had a new attitude toward being Muslim in America: Rather than accommodating to American mores, they wished to maintain a lifestyle consonant with their understanding of Islam. To teach young Muslims about their faith, a growing number of Islamic religious schools, or madrassas, were established in which children could attain both a religious and secular education, such as Catholic parochial schools provide. Over time Muslim students won concessions at a number of private and public schools that have helped them to maintain their Muslim identity. Dartmouth now serves Muslim students halal foods in a designated cafeteria, for example. Many public schools no longer require that Muslim students go to the cafeteria during Ramadan, making it easier for them to observe the fast.

Muslim Arabs arriving since the 1970s have conflicted with the generations of Muslim Arab Americans who laid the foundation of Islamic worship in America. Many recently imported imams, who are unfamiliar with American culture, claim that American Islam must be made to conform to "pure" Islam as it is practiced in most Arab countries. They believe that social functions such as weddings and bake sales should not take place in the mosque, for example. Anthropologist Nabeel Abraham describes the controversy over the role of women in one Detroit mosque, whose leadership passed to recent immigrants: "The new leaders placed restrictions on women entering the mosque. In the past, female members of the congregation were at liberty to enter the mosque as they pleased. After the takeover, they were required to wear head scarves, enter through a special side door, and restrict themselves to designated areas within the building."[6] Khaled Abou El Fadl, a professor at the University of California at Los Angeles School of Law reports, "The immigrant community in the United States tends to be more conservative on the [issue of segregating women in the mosque] than a lot of Muslim countries. Among Muslim immigrants there's a lot of anxiety and insecurity about their Islamic identity, and a lot of it is expressed in ways that are restrictive about women." [7]

Some Muslim women in America are fighting the new restrictions imposed on them by recent Arab and other Muslim immigrants. Citing Islamic history and religious texts, they claim that women have traditionally held an important place in the communal life of the mosque, dating from the time of the prophet Muhammad. While some Muslim women doubt they will be able to make an impact on the entrenched hierarchies of their mosques, others are more hopeful. Nabeel Abraham contends, "It can be expected that the ardor of today's newcomers will eventually wane. Cultural accretions and accommodations will become normal to local Muslims. Gradually, women will assume greater roles in the [American] mosques."[8]

A United Front Against Anti-Arab and Anti-Muslim Hate

World events also created discord within and between Arab American communities. For example, in the 1980s a spate of airline hijackings and other terrorist acts, many committed by Arab terrorists, racked the world. One such incident was the 1988 bombing of Pan American Flight 103 over Lockerbie, Scotland, in which 270 lives were lost. As terrorism became linked in the public mind to Arabs, and all Arabs to Islam, some assimilated Christian Arab Americans no longer wished to identify themselves as Arab. These events did not significantly weaken the unity of the Arab American community, however; in fact, the need to respond to anti-Arab stereotyping strengthened it over time. Arab Americans, whether Christian or Muslim, recognized that they needed to unite to fight anti-Arab and anti-Muslim sentiments and the rash of hate crimes committed against Arab Americans in the wake of terrorist attacks abroad.

Another thing that united Arab Americans of all faiths

was the ongoing plight of the Palestinian refugees (who were themselves a mix of Christians and Muslims) as Israel began to displace them in the territories it had acquired after the Six-Day War of 1967. In order to fight anti-Arab hate crimes, advocate for the Palestinians in a political environment perceived as pro-Israel, and support Arab Americans running for elected office, Arab Americans founded a number of organizations in the 1980s, among them the American-Arab Anti-Discrimination Committee (ADC) and the Arab American Institute .

These organizations were quick to proclaim the loyalty of Arab Americans to the United States in the aftermath of the terrorist attacks of September 11, 2001, and to condemn the attacks. A statement issued by the ADC said, "Arab Americans, like all Americans, are shocked and angered by such brutality, and we share all the emotions of our fellow citizens. Arab Americans view these attacks as targeting all Americans without exception."[9] Like other Americans, Arab Americans lost loved ones in the tragedy and served in rescue units. But unlike their fellow countrymen, they also fell prey to hate crimes and suspicions of complicity. The Arab American Institute found that in the month after September 11, four hundred acts of violence were committed against Arab Americans. These included several murders as well as attacks on mosques. Many Muslim women were afraid to wear their head scarves for fear of attack.

Fears of backlash against Arab Americans subsided when President George W. Bush and other U.S. officials condemned anti-Arab and anti-Muslim hate crimes. Around the country churches and synagogues held interfaith meetings as a way to help their congregations gain a better understanding of Islam and to show support for their Muslim neighbors. Indeed, Americans' thirst for knowledge about Islam skyrocketed after the attacks and Arab American and Muslim organizations took the lead in reaching out to schools and universities, providing speakers and written materials.

More problematic for the Arab American community are the new laws and regulations that have been put into effect by Congress to protect the nation from further terrorist attacks. Among these is the USA PATRIOT Act of 2001, which gives the government broad powers to secretly obtain the records of citizens and noncitizens alike. With the help of the American Civil Liberties Union, the ADC has filed a lawsuit which claims that Section 215 of the USA PATRIOT Act violates the constitutional right of freedom from unreasonable search. Other new laws allow the government to more easily investigate and deport aliens living in the United States. Arab Americans claim that the U.S. government is applying new immigration laws selectively, using a form of racial profiling to single out Muslims and Arabs for special scrutiny. Thus far only alien men of Muslim and Middle Eastern descent have been required to register with immigration officials, and up to nine thousand face deportation for minor discrepancies in their papers. Another complaint is that the U.S. government has targeted mosques in a variety of ways, closing down Islamic charities it claims are tied to terrorist organizations and asking FBI officials to take an official count of local mosques. These measures have made many Arab American Muslims feel like they are being treated as terror suspects, merely for attending their mosques.

A Lasting Legacy

However, despite recent challenges, Arab Americans continue to shape American society as much as they have been changed by it since their arrival in the early twentieth century. Even after the September 11 attacks, Arab American religious life continues to alter the U.S. landscape. Indeed, today Islam is America's fastest-growing religion, with an estimated 6 million followers. Islam is now poised to become America's second-largest religion. While Arab Americans no longer form the largest segment of America's Muslim population, it was Arab immigrants who laid the foundation of Muslim life in America.

Notes

1. Alixa Naff, *Becoming American: The Early Arab Immigrant Experience.* Carbondale: Southern Illinois University Press, 1985, p. 38.

2. Philip M. Kayal, "Arab Christians in the United States," in *Arabs in the New World: Studies in Arab-American Communities*, eds. Sameer Y. Abraham and Nabeel Abraham. Detroit: Wayne State University Press, 1983, p. 52.

3. Joseph Schechla, "The Mohameds in Mississippi," in *Taking Root: Arab-American Community Studies*, vol. 2, ed. Eric J. Hooglund. Washington, DC: American-Arab Anti-Discrimination Committee, 1985, p. 39.

4. Sharon McIrvin Abu-Laban, "The Coexistence of Cohorts: Identity and Adaptation Among Arab-American Muslims," in *Arab Americans: Continuity and Change*, eds. Baha Abu-Laban and Michael W. Suleiman. Belmont, MA: Association of Arab-American University Graduates, 1989, pp. 50–51.

5. Yvonne Yazbek Haddad, "Maintaining the Faith of the Fathers: Dilemmas of Religious Identity in the Christian and Muslim Arab American Communities," in *The Development of Arab-American Identity*, ed. Ernest McCarus. Ann Arbor: University of Michigan Press, 1994, p. 77.

6. Nabeel Abraham, "Detroit's 'American' Mosque," in *Arab Detroit: From Margin to Mainstream*, eds. Nabeel Abraham and Andrew Shryock. Detroit: Wayne State University Press: 2000, p. 280.

7. Quoted in Laurie Goodstein, "Muslim Women Seeking a Place in the Mosque," *New York Times*, July 22, 2004, p. A1.

8. Abraham, "Detroit's 'American' Mosque," p. 303.

9. American-Arab Anti-Discrimination Committee, "ADC Condemns Attack on Trade Center, Government Buildings," September 11, 2001. www.adc.org.

CHAPTER 1

The Troubled Homelands

COMING TO AMERICA

Leaving the Ottoman Empire

Najib E. Saliba

Arabs first left their homelands to settle in America during the last decades of the nineteenth century. At the time most Arabs were subjects of the vast Ottoman Empire ruled by the Turks. The great majority of these early immigrants lived in the Ottoman province of Syria, which today encompasses Jordan, Lebanon, Syria, Israel, and the occupied Palestinian territories. In the following selection Najib E. Saliba describes the conditions that compelled the Arabs to emigrate including a fear of being drafted into the Ottoman army, a lack of political freedom, and the inept rule of the Turks. Whether they resided in the more prosperous regions of Syria, such as Mount Lebanon, or its many poorer areas, Saliba argues that the primary cause of emigration was economics. Saliba, who himself emigrated from Lebanon, is a professor in the history and political science department of Worcester State College in Massachusetts.

The background and causes of emigration from Syria in the last four decades of Ottoman rule will be examined in this article. This period [1880–1922] witnessed the first wave of emigration, an outflow which was interrupted by World War I and, as far as emigration to the United States was concerned, afterwards limited by more stringent U.S. immigration laws.

During most of the period under study, Syria was ad-

Najib E. Saliba, "Emigration from Syria," *Arab Studies Quarterly*, vol. 3, Winter 1981, pp. 56–67. Copyright © 1981 by AAUG and the Institute of Arab Studies. Reproduced by permission.

ministratively divided into three provinces (vilayets) and three autonomous districts called *mutasarrifiyyas* (usually subdivisions of vilayets). . . .

The Mount Lebanon District of Syria

Of all these administrative divisions, that of Mount Lebanon played a pioneering role in emigration. The district of Mount Lebanon was set up as a consequence of a tragedy and was abolished in the midst of another tragedy, World War I. It was established in the wake of European, mostly French intervention in a sectarian civil war in Syria in 1860, during which several thousand Christians perished. The Ottoman sultan, giving in to European pressure on behalf of the Christians, issued a decree setting up Mount Lebanon, an area of about 2000 square miles, as an autonomous district with its governor responsible directly to the Sublime Porte in Istanbul. The governor was to be an Ottoman Catholic Christian but not from Mount Lebanon and was to be appointed by the sultan and approved by the six European powers which guaranteed Mount Lebanon's autonomy. Assisting the governor was an administrative council composed of four Maronite Christians, two Greek Orthodox, one Greek Catholic, three Druzes, one Sunnite Muslim and one Shi'ite Muslim.

From its inception in 1861 to its fall in mid-1915, Mount Lebanon was better governed, administered, policed and its people better educated than the rest of Syria. Many observers noted that its people enjoyed unprecedented tranquility, security and prosperity. They also enjoyed exemption from military conscription and high taxation, two notorious facets of late Ottoman rule. Because of these favorable conditions the residents of Mount Lebanon were envied by their less fortunate neighbors. As the saying went, "Happy was he who had a goat's resting place in Lebanon."

The situation was not totally satisfactory because Mount Lebanon was cut off from its fertile hinterland, the Biqaʿplain, as well as the plains of Sidon and Tyre. Its territory was largely mountainous and little suitable for agriculture. With a high birth rate, little farming and virtually no industry, emigration served as a safety valve to what might otherwise have been an explosive situation.

The relative peace and tranquility which prevailed in Mount Lebanon for over half a century totally disappeared with the onset of World War I. As soon as the Ottoman Empire entered the war on the side of Germany, the Allied fleets [of England and France] blockaded the coasts of Syria and prohibited the importation of all foodstuffs. Local production was not enough to feed the population. In addition, Ottoman military authorities confiscated wheat and other grains in order to assure adequate food supplies for the army. Famine spread all over Syria and hit particularly hard in Mount Lebanon. . . .

Life Was Harsh in the Rest of Syria

If Mount Lebanon enjoyed satisfactory living conditions before the war, the same was not true of the rest of Syria. Although conditions varied slightly from one province to another, public security on the whole was wanting. The people were exposed to the arbitrariness of government officials, the police and tax collectors. There was hardly any security for life and property. Villages at the edge of the desert were constantly exposed to bedouin raids and pillage; urban areas, in turn, suffered from sectarian and other sources of tension. What was the role of government in all this? The government was weak and its intervention could not always be counted upon. High public officials were sometimes unwilling or unable to preserve public order. Insufficiency or inaccessibility of security forces tied the governor's hands. The commander of army troops in a given province did not always work harmoniously with the governor, the highest public official in the province. Furthermore, peaceful relations between the Empire on the one hand and its dissatisfied minorities and the imperial powers on the other were a rarity from 1850 onward. War circumstances invariably led to the withdrawal of almost all security forces from the provinces to the scenes of hostility, leaving the Syrian provinces underpoliced and exposed to lawlessness and domestic strife. At those times public security was obviously at its worst.

The general economic situation also left much to be desired. Ottoman authorities followed a *laissez-faire* [hands off] economic policy. Without official concern and encouragement, agriculture—the cornerstone of the economy—and industry were in a state of decline. Agriculture, for example, had long suffered from neglect, peasant ignorance, pests, inadequate rainfall, bedouin depredation, foreign competition, and dependence on centuries-old methods of farming, threshing and winnowing. Whole villages at the edge of the desert were deserted by the peasants for lack of security and the fields were turned into desert. The annual yield of wheat, barley and maize had progressively fallen. Particularly affected was the cultivation of cotton. Left unprotected from the competition of Egyptian and U.S. cotton, Syrian production of that commodity had practically ceased by World War I.

The situation in industry was hardly better. For years observers of the Syrian economy had noted the decline of the previously vigorous textile industry. Although estimates of the number of workers and looms left in operation varied, there was general agreement that the trend was downward. The problems which hurt the cotton and silk industry the most included high domestic taxation and the lack of protective tariffs in the face of heavy competition by cheap machine-made goods imported from abroad. In addition, a shift in native tastes to European-made clothing led to a shrinking market. The opening of the Suez Canal in 1869 not only hurt Syria's transit trade with Iraq and Iran, it also dealt a serious blow to its silk industry in the international market for it greatly facilitated the transportation of Chinese and particularly Japanese silk to European markets at competitive prices. Syrian silk could not hold its ground. Subsequent attempts to open the American market to compensate for the loss of the French one proved fruitless. In 1889, Syrian production of silk was reported to have been twenty-five percent below that of previous years. Silkworm disease and the cutting down of mulberry trees during World War I accelerated the decline. In the early 1920s, Syria's production of raw silk (cocoons) was little more than one-sixth of what it had been in 1910 (down from 6,100,000 kilograms to 1,300,000). The problems of the textile industry, however, were not unique. The same situation was generally true in other industries such as the production of olive oil and alcoholic beverages, tanning, dyeing, wood engraving and jewelry making.

An already bad economic situation was made worse by the Empire's entry into the war and the establishment of the draft. Males between 18 and 45 years of age were drafted. In a land not accustomed to military service, conscription was very unpopular. Of the 240,000 conscripts about 40,000 were killed and approximately 150,000 deserted. Many others fled their homes and lands to escape the draft. Undoubtedly, this reflected negatively on the security situation, the economy, and, particularly, agriculture.

The number of emigrants from Syria was small, and largely to Egypt, prior to 1878. Emigration picked up steadily in the 1880s and the 1890s and increased sharply in the first fourteen years of this century. There is a virtual concensus among sources that the Christians of Mount Lebanon were the first to emigrate. Although conflicting estimates make it virtually impossible to state with certainty the number of Lebanese who emigrated before 1900, it is estimated that about 5000 emigrants had settled in the United States by 1899 and about 1000 in Canada by 1901. Others went to Australia and the countries of South America. Of a population estimated at 442,000 in 1913, Mount Lebanon had lost more than 100,000 to emigration by 1914 more than one-fourth of its population. It did not take other Syrians long to catch up with the Lebanese. Very soon, emigrants were leaving from Damascus, Jerusalem, Ramallah and the many other towns and villages. By the 1920s, the Syrian community in Egypt numbered over 50,000 of whom more than 15,000 were Orthodox Christians. Probably about 4000 Syrian emigrants had settled in Australia by 1903, over 3000 in Canada by 1921, and some 80,000 to 100,000 in Brazil by 1922. Others settled in Argentina and Mexico.

A large number went to the United States before 1920. It is virtually impossible to accurately determine their number and place of origin in Syria. Part of the difficulty stems from the fact that early Syrian emigrants were entered as Arabs, Turks, Asiatic Turks, and sometimes as Armenians and Greeks in U.S. immigration records. It was only after 1899 that the Immigration Service began to classify such immigrants as Syrians. Even then, the 1910 U.S. census listed no immigrants of Syrian origin in the United States. Following an inquiry, however, another official report put the number of Syrian emigrants who entered the United States between 1899 and 1910 at 56,909.

Why They Left

Although we do not know exactly how many emigrants left, we are much better informed as to why they left. The vast majority left because of economic factors. Whether to Egypt, Australia, North or South America, the main motive was economic betterment. Perhaps foreign missions spread the idea that better economic prospects existed overseas. In the case of Mount Lebanon (unlike the rest of Syria) overpopulation was also an important factor. As already stated, the Lebanese had no access to the fertile plains of the Biqaʿ, Sidon and Tyre. The rest of Syria was unattractive to them because of its economic backwardness and its lack of political and economic security; thus they turned their attention to emigration. The opening of the Chicago fair in 1893 and that of St. Louis in 1906 did much to attract Syrian emigrants. There are abundant references to the importance of those fairs in attracting and spreading immigrants all over the country. Among the Syrian goods displayed were icons, strings of beads and crosses, items for which Palestine was noted. There is hardly any doubt that the general economic backwardness of Syria, the lack of economic enterprise, economic insecurity, ruinous taxation and, above all, the awareness of a better life elsewhere drove the Syrians to emigrate.

Political insecurity and an almost total absence of freedom of expression drove intellectuals to leave. Because of the native and foreign schools which were established in Syria, that country experienced an intellectual awakening in the second half of the nineteenth century. The city of Beirut was the hub of this intellectual activity. Besides its native schools, there was the Syrian Protestant Mission (later known as the American University of Beirut) and Saint Joseph's University. In addition, Beirut was the center of several printing presses, newspapers and magazines. In 1881, the American printing press alone put out 57,500 books, more than two-thirds of which were sold that same year. As a result, a renaissance occurred in the Arabic language. The reading public increased and writers began to discuss serious topics such as better government, social equality, due process of law, improved economy, and improved communications. Stimulating this intellectual movement was the relative freedom of thought and expression which existed in Syria until 1880. However, with the expulsion of Midhat Pasha, a great Ottoman liberal and reformer as governor of the province, censorship was applied to the press and to other forms of intellectual expression. Sultan Abd al-Hamid and his agents gradually squeezed life out of the press and subjected writers and journalists to imprisonment, fines and expulsion. Thousands of books were burned or buried in the ground in an attempt to keep inspectors away.

Faced with tightening Hamidian censorship and economic emaciation at home, Christian and Muslim intellectuals alike fled Syria and took refuge in Egypt, Europe and the Americas. . . .

The Role of Religion

Religious persecution in Syria, particularly the 1860 massacres,[1] has often been cited as a major factor in emigration. The literature dealing with this topic is controversial and not entirely consistent; popular belief and some accounts tend to overemphasize its importance. Sa'id B. Himadeh stated that emigration developed gradually from 1860 to 1900 at an average of 3000 emigrants annually. The American missionary Henry H. Jessup told of a "thousand refugees," presumably Christians, who emigrated to Alexandria aboard a Russian steamer in the wake of the Damascus massacre of 1860. Muhammad Kurd 'Ali, on the other hand, referred to "some" who emigrated to Egypt, Istanbul and elsewhere in the Mediterranean area. An examination of much of the literature dealing with emigration, including accounts written by emigrants, in-

---

1. The 1860 massacres began when Maronite Christians tried to push the Muslim Druze population from the region. The Druze retaliated and up to twenty thousand people lost their lives.

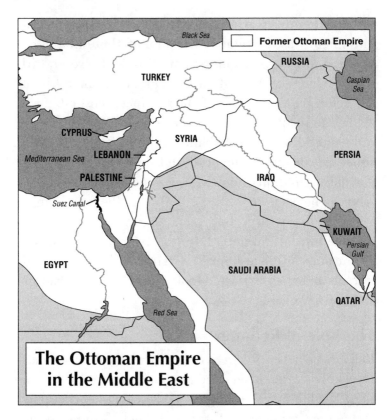

The Ottoman Empire in the Middle East

dicates that, on the whole, religious persecution was a supplementary rather than a primary factor in emigration. While available evidence supports growing emigration from Syria after 1880, there is no convincing proof of a significant and sustained outflow of people in the previous two decades. Hence, the assertion that religious persecution drove Christians to emigrate needs considerable modification and further study. Accounts written by many emigrants do not generally substantiate the persecution thesis for seldom did an emigrant indicate that he had left his homeland because of religious persecution.

Seldom did an emigrant indicate that he had left his homeland permanently. On the contrary, many entertained a desire to return after having made some money. A. Ruppin, a German scholar, reported that one-third to one-half of the emigrants returned and invested their savings in land and in new homes. It is highly unlikely that so many would have returned if religious persecution had been their primary reason for leaving. The fact that sustained and progressive emigration came after 1880, two decades after the 1860 massacres, coupled with the fact that the early emigrants came largely from the autonomous district of Mount Lebanon which had a Christian majority and enjoyed political stability indicates that religious persecution had little to do with emigration. Surely, some emigrants complained of religious fanaticism and bigotry. These complaints, however, followed others such as Ottoman misrule, political oppression, lack of freedom, inequality and lack of economic opportunity. In only one account the case of the Orthodox Christian 'Arbili family, the first Syrian family to come to the United States, is religious persecution named as a primary reason. The 'Arbilis, an upper-class family, witnessed and miraculously survived the sectarian massacres of Damascus in 1860. Having moved to Beirut, a relatively more secure place, Yusuf 'Arbili decided, eighteen years after the massacres, to leave the Ottoman Empire altogether "for the progress of my children." Having been discouraged by the Russian Consul in Beirut from emigrating to Russia, he then turned his attention to the United States.

Religion was an important factor in determining the destination of the emigrants. Most emigrants to Egypt were Muslims and almost all the early emigrants to the West were Christians. Despite the fact that the Christian was usually Maronite, Orthodox, or Melkite, denominations not very common in the Western world, he was still Christian, subscribed to the same basic beliefs, and worshipped and prayed to the same God, and thus could blend into the new society. The Muslim emigrant faced psychological, religious, and cultural obstacles in the West. What would become of him, his children and his religion in the land of the "infidel"? For these reasons the Syrian Muslim, at first, shunned emigration to the West, leaving that option almost totally to the Christian.

Taking Leave

Other factors also influenced Syrian migration. Stories of economic success abroad created a psychological disposition favorable to emigration. The early emigrants themselves, either through correspondence or after an occasional return home, encouraged their relatives and former neighbors to emigrate. Emigration became popular. Some even borrowed the money for their tickets abroad, which cost approximately 230 to 250 francs to South America and 190 francs to New York. Transportation was regular, monthly and sometimes weekly, and emigrants were not encumbered in those days by lengthy forms to fill out, visa applications, and passports or medical examinations. They only needed to go to the port where they could buy their tickets. Agents there often determined their destination for them. Emigrants to the United States took their physical examination before landing at New York City or Boston. The sick were not permitted to disembark and had to return home. In one case, a Lebanese mother and her two children came to join the father who had already settled in Worcester, Massachusetts; the children were not allowed to land because of illness. In another case, a Lebanese was denied entry in 1908 because of trachoma; after returning home, he came back to the United States in 1913. As Ottoman international problems multiplied bringing with them military conscription and a ban on emigration, smuggling thrived with the connivance of high Ottoman officials.

Who were the early emigrants and to what age, sex, or social class did they belong? Evidence indicates that some sixty-eight percent of them were men and the majority of the men (probably sixty percent) were young, unmarried and on the average in their mid-twenties. A small minority were married and perhaps twelve percent of these brought their families with them. The emigration of the young, the unattached, was most serious. Many villages lost their young blood and became shelters for senior citizens. A village in Mount Lebanon called "Bayt Shabab," or the home of youth, later was referred to as "Bayt al-'Ajazah," or the home of the aged!

With the possible exception of the educated minority and the intellectuals, the early emigrants predominately were poor peasants. A very few had some education while the majority were illiterate. As emigrants, they became so absorbed in economic matters that they neglected the world of the mind and failed to avail themselves of the educational opportunities in their adopted country.

The Emigrants Remember Their Homeland

What was the impact of emigration on Syria? Initially, it depleted Syria's manpower, causing a shortage of labor and reinforcing economic stagnation. The loss of the labor force had serious effects on the weaving industry in Mount Lebanon and on agriculture as well. Terraces which the Lebanese peasant had laboriously constructed over the years to preserve his soil lay untended. In the long run, emigration may well have been the cause for the retardation of Syria's economic, political and social development. Not all the consequences of emigration were negative. The emigrants contributed to the relief effort in Syria during World War I and their remittances figured significantly in the economy before the war. In the case of Mount Lebanon, remittances from abroad made up some forty-one percent of its budget by the beginning of the war. Many of those red-roofed houses, so characteristic of the present-day landscape, were paid for with money earned overseas. In addition, the emigrants lobbied extensively for the independence of the modern republics of Syria and Lebanon from France during and after World War II. As that independence was achieved and foreign armies withdrew, both governments initiated serious efforts to tie the emigrants closer to their native land. Soon plans were underway to encourage the emigrants not only to pay annual visits to the "old country" but to invest part of their capital in it as well. Moreover, in the effort to consolidate emigrant Lebanon with resident Lebanon, the Lebanese government has made Lebanese citizenship readily available to the emigrants (who actually never lose their Lebanese citizenship) and to their offspring. They can hold property, public office, and even vote in elections.

A Century of Arab Immigration to Detroit

Sameer Y. Abraham

Metropolitan Detroit is home to America's largest population of Arab Americans. The earliest immigrants were drawn to the region by the opportunity to work in the booming auto factories that burgeoned there in the early decades of the twentieth century. Since the passage of the Immigration Act of 1965, which abolished the use of national-origin quotas, more than four hundred thousand Arabs have arrived in America—among them the Arab elite who came to take advantage of new policies that gave preference to immigrants with professional skills. Many other Arabs came to the Detroit area as refugees, like the Palestinians who were dispossessed of their land following the creation of Israel in 1948 and the first Arab-Israeli war. Other Arabs fled war-torn countries like Lebanon, Yemen, and Iraq. By the early 1990s Detroit's Arab American population was estimated to have reached two hundred fifty thousand. What impresses Sameer Y. Abraham, a sociologist at Wayne State University in Michigan, and the writer of the following selection, is both the national and religious diversity of this thriving population. Since this article was published, many more Iraqis have settled in Detroit following Saddam Hussein's brutal repression of a Shiite Muslim uprising in 1991.

Sameer Y. Abraham, "Detroit's Arab-American Community: A Survey of Diversity and Commonality," *Arabs in the New World: Studies on Arab-American Communities*, edited by Sameer Y. Abraham and Nabeel Abraham. Detroit, MI: Wayne State University Press, 1983. Copyright © 1983 by Wayne State University Press. All rights reserved. Reproduced by permission.

Arab immigration to Detroit (and the United States) can be divided into four broad periods: 1890–1912, 1930–1938, 1947–1960 and 1967 to the present. The Lebanese (Christians) were the first to arrive in Detroit in the 1890s, even though members of this group had already made their way to other parts of the country a decade or two earlier. According to one report, by 1900 there were about fifty Arabs located in the city, consisting mostly of unmarried Lebanese men. While the Christians were among the first arrivals, their Muslim counterparts were not long in following. The first Muslims, in this case Lebanese, arrived between 1990 and 1915, settling in Highland Park near the Ford Motor Company's first factory. Between 1908 and 1913, the first Palestinians (reportedly Muslims) are also reported to have settled in the city, while the first Yemenis made their appearance at about the same time, somewhere between 1920 and 1925, although some reports record their presence as early as 1900. The earliest Iraqi-Chaldean[1] immigrants arrived between 1910 and 1912. Palestinian Christians had already settled in other urban centers as early as 1920.

Subsequent Waves of Immigration

With few exceptions, it is difficult to estimate the size of any particular group of early immigrants. . . . The size of each nationality group and the community as a whole had to be large enough, however, to support the religious institutions which were established during these early years. The first Lebanese Maronite church, for example, was erected on East Congress Street in 1916. Likewise, the first Islamic mosque in America was established in Highland Park in 1919. Both of these institutions testify to the existence of a sizeable Arab population following the first

1. The Iraqi-Chaldeans are Christians whose first language is Chaldean, rather than Arabic. They regard themselves as a minority people, but at times identify themselves as Arab.

wave of Arab immigration in 1890 to 1912.

The second immigration influx between 1930 and 1938 is best characterized as a period of primary growth mainly among Lebanese immigrants. . . .

The third period, 1948–1960, appears to be a primary growth period for all Arab nationality groups, with a marked increase in Muslim immigrants and the entry of Palestinians following the Palestine War of 1948. . . . Unlike the two previous migratory waves, this third wave tended—at least on a national level—to include immigrants who were better educated and more politicized.[2]. . .

With the liberation of the immigration laws in 1965, post-1967 immigration takes a quantitative leap for all nationality groups. Prior to 1965, immigration from the "Asia-Pacific Triangle" (stretching from Pakistan and India to Japan and the Pacific Islands, and including the Arab countries) had been limited to 2,000 persons annually. The abolition of the national origins quota system gave Asian nationals (including Arabs) a more than equal chance to immigrate, although each country was limited to 20,000 persons exclusive of immediate relatives in the United States. The new law took effect on June 30, 1968. Since then Arab immigrants have been arriving into the Detroit area in large numbers, making Arabic-speaking immigrants the fastest-growing immigrant-ethnic community in the area. Arab immigration now spans almost a century; the reasons behind this immigration have changed dramatically for some groups, while for others the causes remain unchanged.

Economic Reasons to Leave the Homelands

Like earlier groups, pre-World War II Arabs migrated to the United States for a combination of reasons, some of

2. Arab immigrants became more politicized following the creation of Israel and the call for a Pan-Arabic movement begun by Egypt's president Gamal Nasser in the 1950s.

which acted as "push" factors whereas others operated to "pull" them in a specific direction. For the earliest immigrants, Hitti suggests that the Syrian-Lebanese immigrated chiefly for economically-related reasons: the destruction of the once prosperous silk industry, limited landholdings on an inhospitable soil, heavy taxation, and occasional drought worked to push the peasantry from the land. On the other side, an expanding American economy was the principal pull force for most early Arab immigrants, whether they were Lebanese, Yemenis, Iraqi-Chaldeans, or Palestinians. Generally speaking, the bulk of Arab immigrants who arrived in Detroit prior to World War II were economically motivated. Their chief objective was to make as much money in as short a period as possible and then return home. The fact that some early immigrants continue to speak of "returning" to their homelands once they have realized their economic objectives is testimony to the fact that many viewed their migration as a *temporary* sojourn and not as a permanent venture.

Economic considerations continued to predominate in the decision to immigrate for Arabs in the post-World War II period as well. As soon as some arrivals established themselves, they sent away for family members and relatives and began a process of "family chain migration" which is still very much in evidence today. With time, it became clear to many immigrants that their temporary status was becoming transformed into a permanent one, either by design or by forces outside their control. Rather than remain alone as single males, they decided to return to their countries to marry or, if married, to send for their wives and children. Assisting family members in immigrating also allowed families to reestablish themselves in North America. Other immigrants aided family members and kinsmen to migrate in order to assist them in family stores and other economic ventures. . . .

Leaving War-Torn Countries: Palestine

The reasons for the post-1967 migration differ markedly from those of earlier periods. While economic objectives remain a major cause for migration, a number of related political factors have intermingled to increase the immigration of all nationality groups during this period. Political and social instability resulting from *coup d'etat*, revolutions, war, and military occupation appear to have accelerated the economic push-pull forces at work. In other words, had these events *not* occurred, it is unlikely that so many Arab immigrants would have decided to immigrate for economic reasons alone.

The two Arab-Israeli wars—1967 and 1973—coupled with the booming oil economies of the Middle East have had a dramatic and far-reaching effect throughout the region and world. These and other events have acted to push immigrants from each nationality group to participate in the largest immigration wave ever to the Detroit area. For the Palestinians, for example, the Israeli military occupation since 1967 has produced a new set of political, economic, and social forces with which the West Bank-Gaza population has had to contend. Major social dislocations have occurred, forcing villagers to quit their lands and homes and travel to other countries in search of education and work. The pressures are increasing on many Palestinians to continue their flight out of the country. While the majority of Palestinians emigrate to nearby Arab countries, a growing number of Palestinians from the West Bank towns of Ramallah, El Bireh, and Beit Hanina are reuniting with kinsmen in the Detroit area.

Civil War in Lebanon

The Lebanese population has faced a similar set of forces, particularly in southern Lebanon. Already economically underdeveloped through decades of neglect, southern Lebanon (and later all Lebanon) became a battleground where the Palestinian-Israeli conflict was fought. Unlike the Palestinians, the Arab-Israeli wars of 1967 and 1973 did not have as momentous an impact on the Lebanese population. Rather, it was the chain of events which followed which produced a major immigrant influx to the United States and other countries of the world (e.g., Greece, France, Jordan). The continuing border skirmishes between Palestinians and Israelis forced many Lebanese to flee to the major urban centers of Lebanon[3] especially Beirut. Border conflict was soon followed by the Lebanese civil war (1975–1978) which divided the country and further debilitated the economy. In the spring of 1978, Israel launched a major military invasion of southern Lebanon against Palestinian guerrillas which culminated in the mass exodus of over 300,000 Lebanese to other parts of the country. While the civil war raged intermittently, inhabitants were fleeing the country in growing numbers. The . . . Israeli invasion of Lebanon (June 1982) and the continuing military occupation of southern Lebanon has exacerbated the situation. Without a resolution to the serious problems of Lebanon and the Palestinians, it is safe to assume that Lebanese emigration will continue unabated. As in the past, some of this emigration will be channeled directly into the Detroit area. In fact, a substantial part of all Arab immigration to the Detroit area can be attributed to the Lebanese situation.

Civil War in Yemen

In the case of the Yemenis, continuing internal unrest after the Republican revolution of 1962 and border conflict between the two Yemens have generated a situation of po-

---

3. Lebanon was host to three hundred thousand Palestinian refugees, some of whom attacked Israel from Lebanese territory. As Israel struck back, Lebanon devolved into civil war, divided about whether or not to support the Palestinians.

litical and social instability.[4] Most of the Yemeni immigrants in the Detroit area originate from the *al-Montaqah
al-Wustah* (the Central Region) in northern Yemen. It is
precisely that area of the country—an area which borders
both Yemens—that much of the border conflict is occurring and where the internal opposition to the existing
regime appears most visible. While political factors alone
are not sufficient as an explanation for continuing immigration to Detroit, these factors coupled with the economic
dislocations both Yemens have faced since the 1960s have
acted to insure that a steady stream of inhabitants would
embark in search of a livelihood elsewhere.

Turmoil in Iraq

As for the Iraqi-Chaldeans, their country faced a revolution in 1958 and a radical change in government in 1968.
The new Baathist government ushered in a set of economic and political policies which set the country on an
entirely new course. Perhaps the most directly destabiliz-
ing event for the Chaldeans has been the attempt by the
Kurdish minority in their area of northern Iraq to win autonomy from the central government. The war between the
government and the Kurds had raged for well over a
decade, until in 1970 a limited form of "autonomy" was
granted to the Kurds. Fighting continued intermittently
but was significantly forestalled in 1975 when the shah of
Iran discontinued his support for the Kurdish insurgents
after reaching an agreement with the Baghdad government
over the division of the Shatt al-Arab waterway. Added to
this are the disastrous effects of the Iran-Iraq war which
began in September 1980 [and ended in 1988]. Even with
Iraq's newly acquired oil wealth, many Chaldeans have preferred to emigrate to the United States rather than con-

4. The two Yemens reunited in 1990.

front the risks of internal instability and a raging war which threatens their area.

The Future of Arab Immigration to Detroit

All in all, it is more than likely that Arab immigration to the Detroit area will continue to increase as long as political stability and sufficient economic opportunity are not present in the countries of Iraq, Yemen, Lebanon, and the occupied West Bank of Jordan. The fact that family members and kinsmen are in the Detroit area both facilitates and provides added incentive for their immigration.

A World Forever Changed: Leaving Palestine

Hisham Sharabi

Civil war broke out in Palestine in 1947 after the United Nations divided Palestine into two states, one for the Jews and another for the Arabs. In 1948 the British, who then governed Palestine, withdrew, and Israel declared itself a nation. The war widened that year when five Arab states attacked Israel in defense of the Palestinians. In this selection from his memoirs, Palestinian-born Hisham Sharabi remembers this time period, when he left his war-torn country to study in America. At that time, he was not greatly concerned with Palestine's fate because he was certain that plenty of young men without the chance to obtain a higher education would join the fight against Israel. With the benefit of hindsight, Sharabi tries to come to terms with his lack of understanding of the magnitude of unfolding events and their aftermath. By the war's end almost two-thirds of the Palestinian population, approximately 750,000 people, became refugees. Sharabi is professor emeritus at Georgetown University, where he taught European intellectual history and cofounded its Center for Contemporary Arab Studies.

We reached the Lydda airport [near Jerusalem] at sunset one very cold day in the middle of December, 1947. The roads were empty except for British armored vehicles. Yusuf

Hisham Sharabi, "Embers and Ashes: Memoirs of an Arab Intellectual," *Post-Gibran Anthology of New Arab American Writing*, edited by Munir Akash and Khaled Mattawa, translated by Issa J. Boullata. Woodbridge, NJ: Jusoor Books, 1999. Copyright

Sayigh's Humber was the only civilian car on the road between Jerusalem and Lydda. He was taking his brother Fayiz
and me to the airport. We were going off to America to continue our graduate studies in philosophy, Fayiz to Georgetown University and I to the University of Chicago.

We had been in Jerusalem the day before, and had
stayed at the Claridge Hotel in Qatamun, managed by a
Lebanese friend of ours. In the afternoon, Joseph Salama
and I went to the Cinema Rex to see a movie, *Habib al-
'Umr* (The Sweetheart of My Life), starring Farid al-Atrash
and Samiya Jamal. We were amazed to find the theater full
of people and life going on as normal, as if nothing at all
was happening in Palestine.

In the little desolate airport, a TWA employee told us
that our flight would be delayed until the following morning. Yusuf Sayigh said goodbye to us and went back to
Jerusalem, and we spent the night at a small hotel in Lydda. That was my last night in Palestine.

The next morning, we boarded our flight. From the
window, I took a long last look at my hometown of Jaffa
[in Palestine]. I saw it from the seaside as we flew over the
ancient harbor. I could clearly see the al-'Ajami neighborhood and the white Orthodox church next to our house. I
thought I could make out our house on the top of al-
'Araqtanji Hill. A few moments later, Jaffa disappeared
from my sight altogether, and I could no longer see anything but the long white shore, and the orange groves that
stretched out behind it to the distant horizon.

Departing While Others Stay On to Fight

I ask myself as I write these words many years later: How
could we have left our homeland while a war was going
on—and the Jews were poised to take control of our country? This question never occurred to me at the time, nor
did it occur to my friend Fayiz. It never seemed strange to

us that Jews of our age group were all in military service, including many young women, nor did we think we should postpone our studies to stay home and fight. There would be enough people to fight on our behalf, we thought. The same people who fought in the 1936 Rebellion[1] would fight for us again. They were peasants who had no need of higher education in the West. Their natural place was on the land. But for us intellectuals, our place was at another level. We fought at the forefront of thought. We were engaged in the bitter and protracted battles of the mind!

I recall an event that took place around the time I left my country. A strong wave of enthusiasm was sweeping through Arab countries towards the end of 1947, brought on by the UN resolution to partition Palestine.[2] [Arab] students at the American University of Beirut demonstrated in the streets demanding to be enlisted as volunteers in the ranks of the Fighters for Palestine (literally the *Army of Deliverance/Jaysh al-Inqadh*). Their request was granted and a large number of them registered at special volunteer centers that had been set up in and around the city. They were told to assemble at Martyrs' Square the next day to be transported to Homs (in Syria) for military training. Out of the hundreds of students who registered, only a very few showed up.

My friend Yusuf Ibish told me about another incident that took place around the same time which involved him and a friend of his. Yusuf was one of the people whose enthusiasm had been ignited by the impending Partition. He and this friend decided to join the volunteers, so they went straight to Damascus, since Yusuf's established and highly respected family was well known there. They went directly

1. Angry at British rule of Palestine and British support for the establishment of a homeland for the Jews in Palestine, the Arabs rebelled—fighting a war that lasted from 1936 to 1939, when the revolt lost momentum.   2. The UN Resolution called for a divided Palestine in which part was reserved for a Jewish homeland and part for a Palestinian state.

to the office of Taha Pasha al-Hashimi, Commander-in-
Chief of the Army of Deliverance, and requested a meeting with him. After a short wait, Taha Pasha received them
very hospitably and offered them coffee. But he categori-
cally refused to let them join the volunteers, saying: "My
sons, fighting is not for young men with your background.
I advise you to return to your classrooms. You are sons of
respectable families. You are educated and can serve your
homeland best by means of learning and acquiring knowledge, not by means of war and guns. Let others who are
more suited for it carry the guns."

The strange thing about it all was that both Fayiz and I

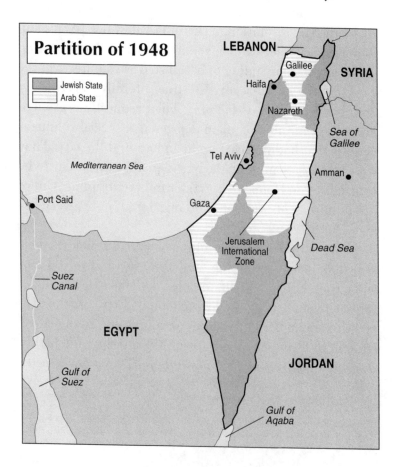

Partition of 1948

- Jewish State
- Arab State

LEBANON

SYRIA

Galilee

Haifa

Nazareth

Sea of
Galilee

Tel Aviv

Amman

Mediterranean Sea

Port Said

Gaza

Jerusalem
International
Zone

Dead Sea

Suez
Canal

EGYPT

JORDAN

Gulf of
Suez

Gulf of
Aqaba

were politically active (we were both members of the Syrian Social Nationalist Party) and had highly developed social consciousnesses. Yet without any hesitation or feeling of guilt we both left our country at a time of severe trial, as if the whole thing were the most natural thing to do, requiring no further thought or reconsideration. In my present efforts to explain this behavior—but in no way to justify it—I find I am at a complete loss. It may be that our education threw dust in our eyes, so that we came to see things from the point of view of abstract thought alone. At the time, the world presented itself to us as the subject of our speech and thought, not as an arena for the realization of our actions. It was enough for us to love our homeland with all our heart and dream of a great future for the nation, without having any obligation toward it other than deep sincerity.

Arriving in America

When the Palestinian shore disappeared from my view, I opened the tray table in front of my seat and began writing the letter which every departing traveler who may never see his homeland again writes—sometimes on paper, sometimes in his heart alone.

Upon our arrival in America, we encountered a blizzard the like of which the country had not seen in a long time. Snow had piled up in New York and Chicago, and all means of transportation were at a standstill. It seemed impossible to get to Chicago from Andrews Air Force Base in Washington where our airplane had landed, and it was already after midnight. But the trains soon resumed their normal schedules, and I left for Chicago, passing through Richmond, Roanoke, and New York. I arrived in Chicago fourteen hours later, traveling hundreds of miles through snow banks piled high on both sides of the tracks.

I took a taxi to the International House on Chicago's

South Side near the shore of Lake Michigan where the University is situated, and as soon as I got out of the car, I heard a voice in Arabic saying: "Welcome to Chicago! The city has lit up at your arrival!" I turned to discover the source of the voice and saw Rashid Fakhri standing at the main entrance with a bright smile on his face. We embraced and entered the building, Rashid insisting on carrying my luggage. I took my room keys to go up to my room and Rashid left me on the understanding that we would meet again after I had some rest.

I entered my room and closed the door. For the first time since I left the airport in Lydda, I was able to think calmly. Here I was in America at last. My dreams had come true. I had arrived at the University of Chicago, and now I was in my private room at the International House. But a feeling of loneliness suddenly overtook me. My heart was about to burst, and my eyes filled with tears. I wanted to go home. I wanted to return to my homeland, to my family, to the Party I had left behind.

A dream realized is like a desire satisfied: it leaves a melancholy void behind it. I decided to return home as soon as possible. I would continue my studies to obtain a Master's degree, nothing more, and go back home within a year—an idea that afforded me a little comfort. I never thought I would spend most of my life in America, and that when I did return to my homeland it would be for only a short and tragic period. . . .

Receiving News from Home

In June of 1948, the first armistice in Palestine was declared. Several months passed by, during which I did not hear from my family. The last news I heard was that my mother and younger brother Khalid were in Acre at my grandfather's. When the Jews later attacked the city, all my relatives escaped to Beirut [Lebanon] and stayed with a lady related to my grandmother, named Khayriyya Hanim, who lived in a small apartment in Ras Beirut near the Shawran Hill. They later moved to a small apartment in the Basta Quarter, on the tramway line. A few months later, my brother Khalid died, and soon after that my grandfather. Only the women remained alive, my mother, my grandmother, my great aunt (my grandfather's sister), and my two maternal aunts. My father and elder brother Nizam were in Jaffa when the Jews attacked it. They escaped to Nablus, my father's birthplace, and they lived there a few months before moving to Amman [Jordan], where they stayed with my uncle Shakib who had been living there before the war.

At first, I didn't realize that what happened to us in Palestine was a blow that greatly differed from all our previous afflictions. All our past had been a chain of misfortunes, but misfortunes came and went, and our lives continued with little change. Now, however, our very roots were torn out and we lost the land our lives were rooted in.

Leaving Egypt

Leila Ahmed

Leila Ahmed grew up in Egypt and attended Cambridge University in England before immigrating to the United States. In the chapter of her autobiography, *A Border Passage: From Cairo to America—A Woman's Journey*, from which this selection is taken, she describes a visit home from England to Ain Shams, a suburb of Cairo. Upon trying to leave Egypt to resume her studies abroad, Ahmed discovers that the Egyptian government refuses to grant her a passport. Until it does, she is forced to resettle for a time in Cairo. Ahmed is convinced that her inability to obtain a passport is the government's method of settling a score against her father, a civil engineer who criticized President Gamal Nasser's scheme to build the Aswan Dam. Nasser came to power after the revolution of 1952, a bloodless coup in which King Farouk of Egypt was deposed. One of Nasser's goals was to redistribute the nation's wealth, thereby creating greater social equality. Ahmed's family was typical of the once-prosperous upper middle class that suffered under Nasser's program of nationalizing private assets. The persecution of political enemies, censorship of the media, and downward economic prospects under the Nasser regime are reasons why many of the educated elite left Egypt in the 1950s and 1960s in search of better educational and professional opportunities in America. Leila Ahmed is a professor at the Harvard Divinity School and is best known for her groundbreaking work *Women and Gender in Islam*.

Leila Ahmed, *A Border Passage: From Cairo to America—A Woman's Journey*. New York: Penguin Books, 2000. Copyright © 1999 by Leila Ahmed. All rights reserved. Reproduced by permission of Farrar, Straus and Giroux, LLC.

I had a job, as good a job as I could get; I was a lecturer at one of Cairo's main universities, the Islamic Women's College, which was part of al-Azhar University. But the pay was low, barely enough to cover the rent for my tiny rent-controlled apartment. I was dependent for everything else—food, clothes, transportation, medical treatment, pocket money—on my parents. It was more bearable, less terrifying to believe that my mother's fears were fantastic, exaggerated than to believe that they really didn't have money and that I was a burden, too great a burden, on them. The terror of not having money is inversely proportional to the remedies and options one has. And if my options and my capacities to go out and earn money in that moment and that society were limited, how much more so were my mother's? What job could she have got?

My having an apartment on my own, a young, unmarried woman, in that society and in those days, I should explain, was itself very unusual and even slightly improper. The situation came about because the Islamic Women's College was in Maadi, a Cairo suburb on the other side of the city from Ain Shams, and so the commute, from Ain Shams by train to Cairo and then by tram to Maadi, was a long one, about two hours. And as it happened—I think none of us would have even considered the possibility otherwise—a flat became available in Zamalek (a central residential district of Cairo) in the same apartment block and right next door to where a close family friend, Madame Sherifa, lived with her two grown children. Her being there helped lend an air of propriety to this enterprise: a responsible older person was close by to keep an eye on me. Yet such was the unusualness and air of slight impropriety that my parents probably would not have agreed to the arrangement had things not been so gloomy at Ain Shams and had they not also been worried about how miserable I was about being unable to leave Egypt. For those were the years that I was trapped in the country, referred from office to office in the Mugammaa, the vast government building dominating the center of Cairo.

And all this, all these obstacles and miseries, were not things that just happened to be occurring—they were being deliberately dealt us, courtesy of the government. "He himself is old and ill? Then get his wife, get his daughter." All this because of some vindictive, malicious person or persons, people who, to curry favor with the *rayyis*, the leader, wanted to punish my father. And for what, what was he guilty of? Speaking out when he was ordered not to by a tyrant? Refusing to be silenced because he feared the costs of his silence would be too great for his country?

All this was happening because we had an unscrupulous government, a government that, in its totally controlled media, spouted an endless rhetoric of liberation, socialism, Arab nationalism, and the Glorious Revolution; a government that ill-treated and abused the rights of its powerless citizens simply because it could.

But these were grim years for others too in Egypt. For one thing, a fair proportion of the people whom my parents knew or who had been part of their broad network of social and professional connections were also in difficult circumstances, also struggling with unfamiliar poverty. Mostly they were people whose properties had been nationalized or placed under sequestration (under government control) and mostly they, too, were elderly people, their children abroad. Socializing now was rare, but it might occasionally happen that I would see at Ain Shams an elderly woman or couple, sitting talking quietly over tea with my mother, and that when they were gone I would hear from her about how this or that person had just stopped taking some heart or other medication because the family could no longer afford it or about how the such-and-such family, living still in its palatial old home because families under sequestration did not have the right to sell property, was now being supported by its chauffeur. The chauffeur lived still in his old room over the garage and shared with his former masters the salary from his job with a newly rich family.

Cairo was full of such stories. These were the years (the late fifties and early sixties) of the Nasser regime's worst repression, when Egypt's prisons bulged with political prisoners—Muslim Brothers and (ironically for a regime that proclaimed itself socialist and was an ally of the Soviet Union) Marxists and Communists. It was a time when Cairo was riddled with *mukhabarat*, the secret police, and their army of informers, ordinary people recruited to report (and eventually rewarded for reporting) any criticism of the government, and it was the era when people suspected of being disloyal to the revolution were being jailed or were disappearing; rumor had it that people could be jailed or disappeared for even the most trivial or oblique comment. Basil, our childhood friend and neighbor, was one such case. He disappeared while doing military service; his mother, desperate to find out what had happened, appealed to the army and the government for information. After two years in prison, he reappeared, the scars of torture on him. He had been in a military hospital after breaking his leg in a parachute jump. One day a radio was blaring in the background when he was trying to sleep, and he called out, "Turn that damn radio down!" It was Nasser making a speech. For those unpatriotic words Basil was thrown in jail for two years, tortured, and beaten.

Stories of government persecution of political enemies, abuse of power, greed, corruption, violence, and general thuggery were rife in Cairo. A man who had disappeared was found by his wife in a garbage bag on their doorstep months later. An officer (and broadly speaking it was the military that was the new class in power) had driven to a grocery store, ordered the owner to fill numerous bags, and driven off without paying. Protesting or disobeying could be costly. People suddenly got rich for no discernible reason, while acquaintances of theirs and sometimes even family members were taken off to prison. Hidayat, a Syrian woman I had met in England, an ardent Arab nationalist and Nasserite, appeared in Cairo and, though a woman of modest means who had never been to Egypt, took up residence in a plush Zamalek apartment. Meanwhile a mutual acquaintance who, in our presence, had been openly critical of Nasser, was in prison. Egyptians abroad knew that they had to watch what they said to other Egyptians—it was well known that Egyptian student bodies in the West were riddled with *mukhabarat*. But it obviously had not occurred to this person—as, until this incident it had not occurred to me—that one needed to watch what one said before other Arabs, too, in this era when Nasser had become the idol of Arab nationalists.

Of course much of this was rumor and speculation; there could be no proof, or no proof that ordinary people could have access to. I myself have no idea which of the rumors were true. But this is a work of memory, not of history, and of the memory of what it was like to live through the aftermath of the Glorious Revolution, rumors and all. An atmosphere of government terrorism was the reality of our world.

Something else happened to the feel of Cairo in those days—as if once you make hatred and derision (that particular derision toward enemies that Nasser was so good at injecting into his speeches) normal and acceptable in one area, they become generalized to everything else. One saw things unimaginable before, small things, details that nevertheless seemed to mark a vast gulf between the old Cairo and this Cairo of the aftermath of the revolution. An old man who just happened to be passing, shuffling slowly by on the pavement, sneered at by two young men simply because he was old: unimaginable before in this society where respect for the elderly was so ingrained and where for the young to address the elderly disrespectfully was something so extraordinary that I had never actually witnessed it. I remember the shock of seeing this now and the feeling I had that I was witnessing the breakdown of a major human taboo. (I know, though, that I cannot succeed in conveying the shock of this scene in a society where the idea that respect for the elderly is a fundamental human value seems weird and not particularly meaningful.) In the old days, too, other people in the street would never have tolerated this behavior; someone would have told those young men off. I remember observing with the same kind of shock as a group of boys threw stones at two women, a mother and daughter, stepping out of an old-fashioned and clearly once-grand car. "Your days are over," they called out, "or don't you know it yet?"

I am not an apologist for feudalism or class privilege or even in some vague way for the old order. I am sure that the revolution brought about many good things and that for other people and in other parts of society doors were opening and new, golden opportunities offering themselves. But not in my neck of the woods.

I know, too, familiar as I now am with the history of many revolutions in our own and in earlier times, that as revolutions go this revolution was very mild in its consequences for political enemies and the old displaced classes. There were no guillotines, no mass executions. And I know that all revolutions bring about justice and liberty and equality first of all and above all for the revolutionaries themselves. The French Revolution executed not only the aristocrats but also those who presumed to ask for a little liberty and equality for their own groups—Olympe de Gouges, for example, executed for the crime of daring to ask for a little liberty and equality for women. And I know that ideals become tarnished and that hordes of small-minded, greedy people ride in on the coattails of revolutionaries, abusing power and further tarnishing the ideals of the revolution. And that in the end leaders come to depend on these sycophants and hangers-on, even if they are not themselves corrupt. There were never, for instance, any rumors in Cairo that Nasser himself was greedy or venal. On the contrary he lived, everyone always said, a simple, even an austerely simple, life. There were rumors that he was vindictive and ruthless toward those that he deemed political enemies, yes, but venal, no.

But this was the only revolution I lived through. Whether I liked it or not, words like *ishtirakiyya, al-wataniyya al-Arabiyya*—socialism, Arab nationalism—and the Glorious Revolution, became for me redolent of fraud. This was not an analytical reaction and I don't believe I even consciously registered it intellectually. It was merely an emotional, lived perception. And the fact is, too, that over these years those people in my experience who took principled stands and who were honest and upright and did not abuse others were not the revolutionaries, not the Nasserites or the Arab nationalists, not the new rich, busily lining their pockets.

CHAPTER 2

Adapting Old Ways to a New World

COMING TO AMERICA

The Americanization of the First Generation

Alixa Naff

The first wave of Arab immigrants in the late nineteenth century settled on the eastern seaboard, primarily in New York City. According to historian Alixa Naff, this first wave Americanized rapidly. In the following article she explains how the immigrants' work experiences and religious practices contributed to their assimilation. Pack peddling, the trade they acquired in the United States, was hard work but had many advantages. It helped the immigrants learn English and enabled them to travel throughout the United States, where they quickly put down roots in many U.S. cities and towns. Other newcomers worked in factories, especially in the burgeoning auto industry of Detroit. Wherever they went, the immigrants published newspapers that addressed their needs as Americans while keeping them in touch with news from their homelands. As the first settlers formed their own communities, they transplanted their religions. Ninety percent of the first wave were Christians who practiced a variety of Eastern-rite faiths, most of which had broken away from Roman Catholicism centuries ago. Others among them brought Islam to America. By the time the Immigration Act of 1924, which established strict national-origin quotas, closed the door to Arab immigration, the Americanization process was so complete that the second generation knew little Arabic. Alixa Naff is the archivist of the Arab American Collection at the Smithsonian Institution in Washington, D.C.

Alixa Naff, *The Development of Arab-American Identity*, edited by Ernest McCarus. Ann Arbor: University of Michigan Press, 1994. Copyright © 1994 by the University of Michigan. All rights reserved. Reproduced by permission.

When villagers began to stream into the Syrian port cities of Beirut and Tripoli,[1] there emerged a host of entrepreneurial and often unscrupulous agents to book steamship passage for the unsophisticated travelers who thought they were headed for New York or at least the United States. Many, instead, found themselves in Canada, South and Central America, the Caribbean, and even Australia. Many of them smuggled themselves across Mexican and Canadian borders, making it further difficult to generate accurate demographic data.

New York and the other ports of entry through which the Syrians entered the United States were merely gateways. Generally, they knew their specific destination and what they were going to do when they arrived there. They were going to pack-peddle merchandise from door to door in towns and cities and from farmhouse to farmhouse in the countryside. They pursued its get-rich-quick potential all over the United States. It was the major magnet that drew Syrian immigrants before about 1910. By that year, they had penetrated every state and territory of the country. They covered the American continent in a network of peddling routes which radiated from a network of peddling settlements. Those few who eschewed peddling because they found it too difficult or too demeaning joined the labor force.

Peddling Settlements

Settlements formed around a supplier—generally a veteran peddler who decided to settle down in a well-chosen location. He would then recruit peddlers from his village or from nearby villages. Kin drew kin and villager drew villager so that immigrants were able to group themselves by kinship, religion, sect, or place of origin as they had in the homeland. Subnetworks of settlements whose members

1. Beirut and Tripoli were in the Ottoman province of Greater Syria. Today they are part of Lebanon.

were mainly from one village can be traced across more than one state. Immigrants of the Druze faith, an offshoot of Shia Islam, had one or two subnetworks of their own.

A peddling settlement was an open and fluid community. That is, peddlers came and went as their self-interest dictated. The supplier's settlement was the peddlers' home base and the supplier their acknowledged leader by virtue of their dependence on him. Yet no special title was attached to him; no abject obedience was demanded. He not only supplied merchandise to the peddler on credit, but guaranteed credit to uncapitalized recruits to induce them to come to him. He received their mail, banked their money, even frequently godfathered their children. He also served as liaison between them and the host community. The good relations between supplier and peddler were based on the canons of tradition and on mutual economic self-interest.

In the settlements the immigrants were taught the rudiments and tricks of the trade by friends and relatives. For example, they were taught the value of U.S. currency and how to address a woman who answered their knock. "Buy sumthin', Maam" was probably the first English sentence they learned. They also learned how to ask for a place to sleep and some food when they were in the countryside. In general, they initially learned how to survive with only a rudimentary knowledge of the language and customs of the country. Consequently, newcomers could start to earn a living almost on arrival. As a near replica of the village, peddlers would return to the settlements to revitalize their spirits after weeks or months on the road.

The Advantages of Peddling

Immigrants were attracted to peddling because initially it required no capital, advanced training, or English-language skills. Moreover, it suited the Arabs' individualist nature and the immigrants' impermanence. Most important, it yielded quicker wealth than they had hoped for.

Peddling was the most fundamental factor in their assimilation for several reasons. It forced them to learn English quickly because learning English was critical to their success; and success, driven by the age-old native competition for family honor and status, was, in the final analysis, the engine that drove Syrians toward their goal in the United States. Peddling further enabled them to see the country and experience its way of life firsthand. It took them into U.S. homes and raised their aspirations. It spared them the uncertainty of finding factory work, standing in long job lines, and industrial layoffs. It spared them, too, a ghetto mentality. Finally, it provided opportunities for thousands of newcomers.

How Peddling Worked

Peddlers were mobile department stores, even when they peddled on foot as most did at first. With well-packed suitcases, frequently one in each hand and one on their back, they carried almost anything a housebound urban housewife or isolated farmwife would need or desire. There were ready-made school clothes, men's work clothes, yard goods, linens, towelling, costume jewelry, and much more. There were also such special items as laces, doilies, crocheted tablecloths, embroidered bedspreads, and ribbon-decked dusting caps frequently made by the women in the peddler's family in a kind of settlement cottage industry.

In the notions case, which was the peddlers' primer and constant companion, were all the kinds of notions one would find at a Woolworth's notions counter plus icons, frames, rosaries, etc. If the peddlers' hands were full, the notions case dangled on his chest.

Some peddlers covered half a continent on foot and remained away from the settlment for months; others returned in a week or two, while usually, but not always, women and children remained closer to the settlement.

Peddling was a hazardous occupation. These villagers, accustomed as they were to hardships in their villages, never reckoned on what they would encounter on the road in the United States. Their hardships are preserved in a body of humorous anecdotes that glorify cunning and ingenuity, and which acted as a psychological safety valve for their fear, fatigue, and frustration when they told them to each other. Many of the anecdotes deal with the hardships of climate, lack of knowledge of the language, and the difficulties of finding lodging. They tell about frozen extremities, parched throats, relentless heat; of being mired in mud, robbed, beaten; of killings and being lost; and of being chased by farmers with guns and dogs. "How do you tell a dog to go away if it doesn't understand Arabic?" complained an informant. One peddler, articulating the consensus, said that he "endured a lot" but enjoyed this country and he was "free to make money."

Peddlers did indeed make money. As a whole, they averaged $1,000 annually when the U.S. labor force was averaging about $650 annually. High earnings and unrelenting frugality allowed them to send remittances home, pay debts, and buy fares to bring other family members to the United States. They contributed to U.S. commerce by expanding the market of small industry products to the most remote areas of the country.

By about 1910, peddling declined as an immigrant occupation. Immigrants had outgrown it, and its services to U.S. consumers were replaced by proliferating department stores and mail-order houses such as Montgomery Ward and Sears Roebuck.

Factory Workers and Entrepreneurs

When immigrants decided to settle down and make the United States their permanent home, they adhered to the cherished cultural ideal of being in business for one's self. They turned to family businesses in which the whole family participated, even the young. Usually, the home and the store were a staircase or a door apart. Dry goods and grocery stores were most popular, but businesses ran the gamut from banking and wholesaling and manufacturing to movie houses, pool rooms, confectionery stores, and dry cleaning. With little or no experience in most of these endeavors, failure was common but not daunting. They simply kept trying until they succeeded.

Many immigrants who arrived in the period of peddling's obsolescence and afterward in the 1920s entered the labor force. They were attracted by industry's payment of five dollars for an eight-hour day, which was initiated during the war by the Ford Motor Company and adopted by other manufacturers. This innovation coincided with the influx of Syrian Muslims. Yet many of the men who worked on assembly lines also opened stores which were operated by their women relatives and children.

The Americanization process advanced most rapidly after World War I. Settlements, generally located in ethnically mixed low-income neighborhoods, ultimately matured into stable communities as immigrants bought homes and acquired middle-class symbols such as home appliances and cars. In general, they followed the middle-class path up the economic and social ladder. Moreover, they adopted the respective regional social attitudes, tastes, and accents and became New Englanders, Southerners, Midwesterners, etc.

Transplanting New Faiths

The ethnic institutions which they established—churches, an Arabic-language press, and voluntary associations—not unexpectedly reflected the traditional identity factors and perpetuated the traditional community fragmentation.

The first churches were of the Eastern-rite faiths.[2] Most prominent among them were the Maronite, Melkite, and Eastern Orthodox. There was also a Syrian Protestant church. These were built in the early 1890s in New York City which was the Syrian mother colony and the cultural and economic center. Churches increased slowly and unevenly across the country in the next half century. Nevertheless, vast areas were, and remain, unserved. Syrians in these areas, therefore, attended "American" churches, that is, Roman Catholic and Protestant. This accounts, in large part, for the relatively high percentage of mixed marriages before and after World War I. Syrian identity in these households, even more so in those of their descendants, was consequently diluted.

The accelerating assimilation of Syrians reduced attendance at all Eastern-rite churches. In order to arrest the defection, to reach the nonspeaking offspring, and to perpetuate the unity of the subgroup, the leaders acknowledged the inevitable. Liturgies were anglicized and shortened, chants were westernized, and choirs replaced cantors.

Americanization of the Maronite and Melkite churches had begun very early because, as affiliates of the Roman Catholic church, they came under the administrative authority of the church in the United States. Consequently, Maronite and Melkite churches served by their own clergy spread very slowly until their independence from Roman Catholic authority after World War II.

On the other hand, the Eastern Orthodox church turned for guidance in the United States to the Russian Orthodox archdiocese. The latter, in turn, ordained the first Syrian bishop in the United States. A year after his ordination in 1904, he established a cathedral in Brooklyn. Un-

2. Eastern-rite faiths are distinguished from the Church of Rome by their history and religious practices. These differences resulted in the Great Schism of 1054, when the Churches of Rome and the Byzantine Empire officially divided.

der his leadership, Orthodox churches increased and many adherents returned to their native faith.

Only in four Muslim communities were mosques known to have been built before World War II. Yet Muslims fulfilled their spiritual obligations without fear of perdition. For Muslims, any uncontaminated place at home or work could be a place to pray. Both Muslims and Druze immigrants could compensate for lack of consecrated religious institutions by gathering for prayer, reading from holy books, discussing religion, or celebrating religious festivals.

Clubs and Societies Foster Group Identity

The traditional identity factors prevailed in the Arabic-language press and in the formation of clubs and societies. It was in the United States that Syrians learned to organize around a common purpose or cause. They developed such a propensity for it that at any given time, the number of organizations was out of proportion to the number of Syrians in the United States. Most, of course, were short-lived.

Family, religious, and village social clubs proliferated in part to counter the rate of mixed marriages and to maintain the continuity of the subgroup. If these clubs had a central and common theme, it was the underlying one of group solidarity mainly through in-group marriage. They tended, therefore, to be exclusivist. Attempts by the U.S.-born Syrians to change this divisive custom succeeded only after World War II. . . .

A Proliferation of Arabic Newspapers

An active and highly competitive Arabic-language press was centered in New York City. The impetus for its development was provided by the immigration of a few intellectuals who were graduates, for the most part, of religious and secular schools of higher education in the cities of Syria. It was coincidental and fortuitous that in New York the publishers of newspapers and journals, many of whom had had little or no prior journalistic training or experience, came together with émigré Arab writers and poets in a symbiotic relationship to form an immigrant intelligentsia.

The Syrian penchant for publishing matched their penchant for organizing clubs and societies. Dailies, weeklies, and monthlies appeared and disappeared regularly between 1892 and 1930. Yet the press was influential and contributed significantly to the Americanization process. From its inception it explained the U.S. social, economic, and political life to its eager readers, albeit in fairly simple and idealized terms. It tied success to becoming "American", and encouraged and taught good citizenship. In addition, it kept immigrants informed about events in the homeland. Many Syrian immigrants became informed, for the first time, about the society, politics, history, literature, and culture of Arabs in general and Syrians in particular. Never before had these predominantly village centered, poorly schooled readers learned so much about their heritage even though it was filtered through sectarian biases. Having befriended the intellectuals, Syrian publishers from the start used the pages of their publications to launch, test, and advance the early literary output of a school of modern Arabic literature in the United States which was to revolutionize age-old Arabic literary forms.

Only three of several influential newspapers survived into the post-World War II period. *Al-Hoda*, published six years after *Kaw-kab Amrika*, the first Arabic-language newspaper, appeared in 1898, and spoke for the Maronite community. *Meraat al-Gharb*, the voice of the Syrian Orthodox and of anti-Ottoman Arab nationalists, was launched in 1899 to oppose what its publisher considered to be the political and religious biases of *Al-Hoda*. *Al-Bayan*, not published until 1911, spoke for the Druze and Muslim community although it was started by a Druze.

To its own detriment, the Arabic press, for all its complaints against fragmentation of the community, succeeded, in effect, in exacerbating the divisions. Moreover, by establishing itself on a sectarian basis, its respective publications did not address themselves objectively to the interests of the broad readership, thus limiting that readership.

Ancestral Roots Are Left Behind

The appearance in 1926 of *The Syrian World*, a monthly opinion and literary journal in English, signified the publisher's recognition of the end of an era as well as a crisis in the use of Arabic. It was aimed at the U.S.-born generation which could not read Arabic, the generation that the publisher, Salloum Mokarzel, called the Syrian-American generation. The immigration quota act limited the entry of Arabic readers and speakers at the same time that the accelerated Americanization process was eroding the use of Arabic. English increasingly replaced the native language in the homes and at the social functions of immigrants and those of their married children. Attempts by community leaders to teach Arabic to their offspring who were products of U.S. schools and ardent consumers of such innovations as moving pictures and radio programs were defeated by the pace of assimilation. The usefulness of Arabic publications, therefore, declined, as did their numbers.

The impact of the Americanization process was most evident in the family and most significantly in the role of women. Women gained greater self-confidence and a sense of independence as they assumed responsibilities traditionally performed by the patriarch of the household. Their increased participation in the economic welfare of the family as well as in more disciplinary and decision-making responsibilities led to the gradual eroding of traditional social restrictions on women—mainly in the Christian community.

Rapid Americanization did not, however, prevent parents from inculcating their children with an important and, it seems, ineradicable set of traditional values. Most notably among them were strong family units, upholding the family honor, improving its status, and adhering to the family's religious beliefs. These core values drove the Syrians to achieve their primary goal in the U.S. and gave rise to corollary values which proved to be compatible with the most cherished U.S. values: self-denial, thrift, initiative, perseverance, individualist attitudes, and a strong work ethic.

In their eagerness to succeed, the immigrant generation neglected to preserve their cultural heritage. Much of what that generation knew of their heritage was, in any case, centered on village life and its mythology. About the great Arab-Islamic contributions to world civilization the majority of the immigrants knew little, and what they did know was selective and refracted through traditional biases.

This village view of Arab culture left immigrant children poorly informed about their deeper historical roots. They knew little of the kind of events that in other nations produced national heroes and kindled ethnic and national pride. The void, therefore, was filled from the well of American myth and history. As a further consequence, the American-born and American-raised generations showed scant interest in or knowledge of their ethnic origins. References to Arab or Syrian culture were as remote as their parents' homeland. If the political events in the post-World War II Arab World had not reactivated Arab immigration and provoked the descendants of the first wave into an Arab identity, they might have assimilated themselves out of existence.

New Identities and Old Traditions: Advice to Syrian American Youth

W.A. Mansur

The *Syrian World* was a newspaper first published in 1926. By this time the first generation of Arab immigrants had given rise to a second generation of native-born English-speaking children. The *Syrian World* was thus published in English rather than in Arabic. Unlike other Arab American publications of its day, the *Syrian World* addressed all Arabs regardless of their religious affiliation. It thus attempted to unify the Syrian community in America and strengthen its solidarity. While helping them to adjust to life in America, the paper kept immigrants and their offspring in touch with news from their homelands. In 1927 the Reverend W.A. Mansur wrote a series of articles about the problems of Syrian youth in America, in which he addressed the difficulties they faced holding on to their heritage while assimilating to life in America. One problem these youth confronted was prejudice due to the religions they practiced, such as Eastern-rite Christian traditions and Islam, which were then little known in America. The reverend urged his readers to become patriotic U.S. citizens but also to maintain pride in the traditions of their forefathers and to earn an education.

W.A. Mansur, "Problems of Syrian Youth in America," *Syrian World*, vol. 2, January 1928, pp. 9–14.

Essential to the happiness, welfare and progress of Syrian-American youth, their posterity and their race,[1] is an intelligent understanding of the meaning of American patriotism, citizenship and government. As immigrants we have made the supreme decision to make America a permanent home. We owe it to America, to ourselves and posterity to become Americans.

The American Republic is founded on fundamental human rights without regard for color, creed, race, station or previous condition. America's principles are coterminous with human freedom, happiness, liberty. [President Theodore] Roosevelt said, "Americanism is a matter of the spirit and of the soul." Americanism expresses humanity's yearning for independence and freedom, political, religious, educational and otherwise. American patriotism is native to Syrian nature, character, and aspiration.

Do Not Be Ashamed of Who You Are

What America does not ask is as important as what she does ask of new Americans. She does not ask that you forget and not love the land of your early humanity; that you refuse to acknowledge your race and your love of your race; that you feel a sense of shame because of early material poverty; that you lose your love for the language of the homeland; that you make no reference to the talents and achievements of your race and homeland; that you see no beauty in the customs of your people.

What does American patriotism mean? Certainly not party affiliation. Rather that you put America first in your thinking: politically, religiously, educationally. That you believe in, uphold, and defend the Constitution of the United States. That you believe in the "larger Patriotism".

1. In the early 1900s pseudo-scientific theories of race (which assumed that some races were superior to others) were prevalent. Today we would use the term *ethnic group* instead of race to refer to national or religious identity.

Roosevelt said, "The larger patriotism demands that we refuse to be separated from one another along lines of class or creed or section or national origin; that we judge each American on his merits as a man. . . ."

American patriotism also means that you remember that the American nation is composed of immigrants. . . . The only difference among Americans is that some came earlier while others came later, indeed as it were yesterday to these shores. The only original American is the Indian. This historical fact should be forever borne in mind. . .''

How to Practice Your Faith in America

Religious nature reached its highest under Syrian skies. Atheism, agnosticism, infidelity, are foreign to Syria and Syrians, be they Mohammedans, Christians, Druzes or Jews.[2] Religion is constitutional and a practical need. Out of human hearts and experience arose faith in God. Man lived the religious life and then went about constructing arguments for his beliefs. As man's knowledge develops, his needs increase, so does God's revelation.

Syrian religious thinking is open to the new knowledge in science, education, religion, so long as it is knowledge. Tolerance of religious faith and worship are native to Syrian thinking. The reformation spirit was born in Antioch, Syria, with Paul,[3] and was carried to Europe, and, in time, reached America. . . .

Reconstruction and restatement of religious beliefs is inevitable. Syrian-American youth need guidance. . . .

Syrian-American youth are baffled by the numerous religious denominations: the result of freedom of religious thought and worship. . . .

2. For centuries Syria was home to the three monotheistic faiths of Judaism, Islam, and Christianity. The author refers to *Mohammedans*, a term mistakenly used in the nineteenth century to refer to Muslims. The Druze are an offshoot of Islam.   3. The Eastern-rite Christian religions of Syria date back to the time of Paul and the apostles.

First, believe your beliefs, doubt your doubts. Syrian-American youth receive sufficient religious and moral training at home to worship God and love mankind.

Second, attend the church of your fathers and do not coquette [flirt] with other denominations, unless you are capable of adjusting your religious beliefs.

Third, rise above the prejudice and undignified attitude toward you. . . . Attend religious institutions where you will be regarded with respect and taken in on equal terms.

Fourth, beware of religious indifference. It blights and often kills the soul. The bedlam of religious voices brings on the I-don't-care spirit. You owe it to yourself to attend to your soul's need. Religion was a national and racial inheritance, it is becoming a personal matter and based on personal choice and achievement.

The separation of church and state is essential to human freedom. Syria and Syrians for ages longed for liberties we now enjoy.[4] It's ours to tend the gates of liberty. Beware of prejudice, intolerance, ignorance, superstition, autocracy, anything which shackles human hands, hearts, minds. America's constitution does not abrogate religious liberty, it requires that free men shall worship God according to their consciences, and that government shall derive its authority from the consent of the governed without coercion: religious, political, educational. . . .

Become Well-Educated

Little schooling is another danger to guard against. The *New York Evening Post* says, "Eighty-five per cent. of all children who enter the first grade in school have to go to work before they reach the eighth grade. The average length of schooling in the United States today is less than six years."

---

4. Syria had been a part of the Ottoman Empire ruled by the Turks up until the end of World War I.

Education pays in many ways. Dean Everett W. Lord of Boston University College of Business Administration says that an untrained worker in the years between 14 and 60 may earn about $45,000; a high school graduate between 18 and 60 may earn about $78,000; and a college graduate between 22 and 60 may earn about $150,000.

Many are the results of education. It develops our capacities, often with a revelation of suspected talents in us. It reveals life in its broader aspects, helping us to live sanely, soberly, successfully. It gives depth to our convictions, and a broader foundation to our faith. It enlarges our minds and hearts, multiplying our enjoyment of life. It increases our earning power and our capacity for unselfish world-service. It gets us in touch and possible possession of the treasures of the past.

If you would be educated read good books. Good books inspire the mind, enlarge our vision, stimulate ambition. You will think, know, and grow in mind and heart. Read biography, history, poetry, science, philosophy. If you can read, you have no excuse for not getting an education. The public library is the best university of the common people.

Syrian-American youth are acquitting themselves in splendid achievement. *The Syrian World* is reporting evidences of this fact. The Syrian racial intellect matches with the highest of other races. It is free in America and elsewhere to vindicate its claim to a place of high leadership in religion, education, commerce, science, and otherwise.

Syrian-American youth, I challenge you to the best in your racial possession. . . .

A Stronger Group Identity

The realization of the problems of Syrian-American youth has brought about certain adjustments. It has called for a coming together of Syrians from outlying places. It has called for a literature on Syria and Syrians. It has created a new outlook on the part of Syrian parents. It has created a new racial solidarity. It is uniting scattered families through marriage ties and other social needs. It is laying a foundation for a growing Syrian people in America. It will serve to raise the confidence of Syrians in themselves, their children, and their race. It will give courage to withstand the onslaught of race, color, and creed prejudice. It will arouse sympathy for fellow Syrians who have like problems. It will bring fellow Syrians to the assistance of a distressed worthy Syrian brother, be he Mohammedan, Christian, Druze or Jew.

The intelligent understanding of certain social problems by Syrian-American youth, the better methods of their solution, and the social racial consciousness that pertains to them, will enlighten their minds, give them principles for daily living, and strengthen their minds and hearts as they face the future and success.

Practicing Islam in America

Yvonne Haddad

In the following article historian Yvonne Haddad explores the ways Arab Muslim immigrants have practiced their religion in America. Arab Muslims represented only 10 percent of the first wave of Arab immigration, which ended in 1924. Nonetheless, this generation established mosques in a variety of places beginning in the 1920s, such as Highland Park, Michigan; and Michigan City, Indiana. Haddad explains that although many Muslims married outside of their religion, others established the foundations of Muslim worship in the United States while at the same time assimilating to American lifestyles. After World War II Muslims represented 60 percent of Arab immigrants. In the 1950s and 1960s these newcomers tended to be the secularized Arab elite, but Arab Muslims arriving since then have brought with them a new religiosity as well as the practice of more traditional forms of worship. This return to tradition has included a desire to limit the mosque to religious functions and to exclude a variety of social functions it had acquired in America. As Haddad describes it, this movement has caused conflict within some Arab Muslim communities, especially over the proper role of women in the mosque. Haddad is a professor of the history of Islam and Christian-Muslim relations at Georgetown University.

As in other areas of the world, the initial growth period of Islam in North America reflected "mixing" or acculturation. Severed from traditions accumulated over centuries, the immigrants attempted to create their own Islamic institutions. For this, they borrowed institutional forms from the local inhabitants. The role of the mosque in North America is closer to that of denominational churches than to mosques in the Arab world.

The Americanization of the Mosque

Historically, the mosque has functioned as a gathering place for the community, where Muslims expressed their religious and political allegiance during the Friday service.[1] In the new country, it acquired a social and cultural meaning as the Arab Muslims struggled to maintain an Arab and Islamic identity in an alien culture. Not only are wedding and funerals conducted at the mosque, in keeping with American practices, but even fund-raising activities (primarily directed by women) such as mosque bazaars, bake sales, community dinners, and cultural events have been adopted as well. Occasionally, even folk dancing in the basement of a mosque has brought young people together in fellowship.

Women participate in other aspects of mosque life generally not open to them in the Middle East. These include attending the Sunday service and teaching Sunday school. Interviews with second- and third-generation Muslims indicate the very active role assumed by pioneering Arab Muslim women in the construction and maintenance of the mosque. This role has been curtailed in areas where more recently arrived immigrants predominate. A coalition be-

---

1. Devout Muslims pray five times a day facing Mecca. These prayers need not be said in a mosque. On Fridays, however, Muslims are enjoined to pray in a mosque as part of a community. There an imam, or worship leader, leads the prayers and offers an address to the community. This congregational worship is called *jum'ah*.

tween illiterate traditional rural men and highly educated young students or immigrants committed to a strict Islamic order has formed, and, as one third-generation Arab-American Muslim put it, appears to be operative in "wresting the leadership of the mosque" away from those who labored long to bring it into being. In an increasing number of Arab Muslim mosques where traditional imams[2] have been installed, women have seen their participation in mosque functions reduced and restricted, a restructuring aimed at conforming to patterns idealized in the Arab world.

Also reminiscent of Christian practices is the passing of the collection plate (witnessed in Quincy, Massachusetts) during the Sunday meeting to supply funds for the maintenance of the mosque.[3] Sunday services and Sunday schools have been adopted as a result of adjustment to North Americans' realities. Most working members cannot attend the prayers on Friday, which is the designated day for communal worship in Islam.

The manner in which the mosque is administered also reveals a distinct American influence. There is a predominance of "congregational" control in the mosque, as elected committees have assumed the right to hire an imam or prayer leader. In the Arab world, most mosques are controlled by the ministry of endowments, giving local people no power in matters of administration. With the appointment of imams financed by outside sources, such as Al-Azhar[4] in the 1960s and the Muslim World League [an international organization founded in Mecca in 1962] at present, local congregations appear to have lost some of their powers. The bureaucratization of Islamic Institutions

2. The imam leads congressional worship in the mosque. While the imam in Sunni Islam is a learned individual, he is not part of an ordained or hierarchical clergy.   3. Muslims support their mosques and other charitable institutions by fulfilling the duty of Zakat, the fourth pillar of Islam. These funds (calculated as a percentage of one's wealth) would not be donated on a collection plate in a traditional mosque.   4. Al-Azhar in Cairo, Egypt, is among the most prestigious universities and Islamic training centers in the Muslim world.

under umbrella organizations appears to act as deterrent to acculturation and Americanization. . . .

The Changing Role of the Imam

The role of the imam in the larger mosques has taken on added significance, given the new realities of the American milieu. The traditional duties of leading the community in prayer and providing guidance through preaching and Quranic exegesis [explanation of the Koran] have been expanded to include the administration and maintenance of the mosque. Moreover, the minority status of the Muslim community has added to the imam's duties, which now include attending to the community's general welfare as well as representing them in interreligious functions. He has become the spokesman for the group, the ambassador of the Muslims to the community, frequently lecturing about Islam in churches and schools.

Another feature of the imam's new role is his function as a family guide and counselor. With no training in counseling, the imam often reverts to providing Islamic answers based on theological law, which is not received favorably by some members of the second- and third-generation Arab Muslims.

The predominance of nuclear families among Arab Muslims has led to undue pressures on the spouses who are accustomed to the counsel of friends and relatives. Arab customs relegate problem-solving to parents or an inner family circle, who arbitrate conflicts and function as peacemakers. The absence of such help in the United States places great stress on the couple, allowing misunderstandings to fester and continue unresolved. Imams in various cities have reported that their help is generally sought as a last effort, given the tendency of Arabs to confine the knowledge about intimate affairs to the immediate family.

Imams are also pressed into upholding the traditional

morality[5] by the older generation, a demand that keeps a substantial number of Muslims away from the mosque. The freedom to choose from a multiplicity of lifestyles, with no clearcut societal definition of acceptable behavior, is upheld by second-, third-, and fourth-generation Arab Muslims as part of being American. In many ways, these lifestyles contradict the traditional Islamic legal and cultural patterns. The fact that imams are trained in the Arab world and have little understanding or tolerance for American customs leads to further alienation of the American-born.

Interfaith marriage, especially in cases where the woman does not convert to Islam, has led to deep strains in marital relationships. This is particularly true with regard to the religious education of children. The liberal Muslim father who advocates and practices permissiveness tends to become more inflexible when the religious instruction of his children is involved. The imam thus plays a primary role both in helping families resolve some of the problems attendant to these concerns, and in providing the kind of Islamic education desired by many Muslim parents.

In the smaller and more recently established societies, the role of imam is assumed by the most learned man in the congregation. Sometimes, he is the one most thoroughly versed in Islamic traditional learning; in other instances, he is often the person who has earned the highest academic degree. Both forms of leadership may exist in the same congregation, so that one leads the prayer while the other preaches the sermon or becomes the president of the executive committee.

The Mission of New Immigrants

Since the beginning of the 1970s, there has been a return to normative Islam, sometimes referred to as "reform." Ef-

5. One of the greatest areas of conflict between traditional Islamic practice and American culture concerns premarital dating.

forts are made to purge Islam of innovations which accumulated over the years and to eradicate unnecessary and
un-Islamic patterns of acculturation. . . .

The dramatic increase in the number of Muslims in the
United States . . . has heartened followers who remember
a time when Muslim holidays went by scarcely noticed or
observed. The celebrations in the various mosques and organizations have added a new dimension to the growing
sense of dignity, identity, and purpose of the Muslims. . . .

The affirmation reflects the growing belief of Muslims
that they have a purpose and a message for mankind. The
sense of mission in the United States is nurtured by Muslim scholars from India, Pakistan, and Saudi Arabia, who
travel throughout the country proclaiming normative Islam, and by various local Muslim organizations which are
committed to *daawah* (mission) and supported by mission funds from Saudi Arabia, Kuwait, Qatar, Libya, and
Pakistan. . . .

This does not mean, however, that Islam has an easy
task in the United States. Even among immigrant Muslims,
mosque participation is limited. Community observers estimated that between one to five percent are active mosque
participants. The number is higher in some areas where
family chain migration is pervasive, or where the Arab
Muslim group is relatively stable and there is no steady influx of new immigrants.

Social class, national origin, level of education, focus of
identity (whether national or Islamic), and ability to integrate in the American society appear to have direct bear-
ings on mosque attendance. These factors also affect conflict in the mosque. Arab Muslims reflect the political,
ideological, and territorial differences of the countries
from which they emigrated. These differences sometimes
become a major focus of contention among individuals affirming exclusive claim to their view of the "true" Islam.

A substantial number of un-mosqued are disaffected by the conflict. Others find the reforms to be irrelevant to life in America. Still others are well-integrated second-, third-, and fourth-generation Americans who resent outsiders telling them what to do. They are alienated from the recently arrived who take religion "very seriously," making themselves noticeable and open to possible discrimination by the host society. Among those in the un-mosqued ranks are the professional and intellectual Arab Muslims who arrived in the 1950s and 1960s. . . .

Obstacles to Muslim Worship in America

The early immigrants faced grave problems establishing Islam. Mostly uneducated and unacquainted with American culture, they felt discrimination in their jobs as well as in their efforts to erect houses of prayer. Zoning laws sometimes obstructed them. They found themselves unable to teach Islam to their children for want of materials in English.

Muslims are also hampered in fulfilling their prayer obligations which require praying five times a day at prescribed times, including noon and early afternoon, because they often face ridicule or pressure from their peers. The author is aware of one Muslim who lost his job because he was performing ablutions (the necessary ritual cleansing of hands, feet, elbows, ears, face and head before prayer) in the men's room. Prayer also requires a clean area with no pictures or portraits hanging on the walls.

Muslims are expected to join other believers in the communal prayer on Friday, an impossibility for many. Consequently, communal prayer services held on Friday are often attended by the old and unemployed. Almost all mosques hold Sunday services, which serve only as alternative meetings and do not replace Friday worship.

The two most important holidays of Islam, *Eid al-Fitr*

(celebrated at the end of the month of fasting) and *Eid al-Adha* (observed by Muslims worldwide at the end of *Hajj*, the pilgrimage to Mecca where the whole community of Muslims renews its dedication to the worship of God) are not recognized holidays in this country (except in Dearborn, Michigan where the holidays are recognized semi-officially). Muslim students are not excused from classes, nor are workers given a day off to participate in these celebrations.[6]

The dietary laws of Islam forbid the consumption of alcohol, pork, and improperly slaughtered meat. Muslims are expected to eat *halal* (meat from an animal that is not stunned, but properly butchered and bled with the name of God recited at the time of slaughtering). Some urban areas have butchers who sell *halal* meat. Other Muslims use Kosher meat, reciting the proper phrase on it before consumption. But most Muslims have no access to *halal* butchers. . . .

Muslims often see overindulgent, materialistic American culture as opposed to the Islamic ethos. The Quran teaches that man was placed on the earth to administer it for God. The emphasis on consumption and planned obsolescence is paramount to mismanagement of resources; the goals of individualism and personal gratification jeopardize the Muslim teaching of communal commitment and responsibility. Individual satisfaction leads to exclusiveness and discrimination which are contrary to the revelation of the Quran affirming that all people are brothers and sisters. The only way one human being can excel over another is in piety and devotion to God.

Islam has faced other problems in America. A logistical problem arose as Muslims scattered throughout the

---

6. In recent years schools and colleges across America have made greater accommodations for the needs of their Muslim students. During the fast of Ramadan many schools now excuse Muslim students from the lunchroom and provide them other spaces in which to meet. Some universities are offering *halal* (or ritually blessed) foods.

United States. Although the number of mosques and Islamic centers continue to increase, the dispersal speeds the process of acculturation and Americanization and leads to local innovations. Where chain migration has occurred in cities like Cedar Rapids, Detroit, Toledo, and Quincy, the Muslims were able to organize institutions early. Family ties, shared experiences, and common outlook helped weld the community together. The second and third generations, while committed to their Arab Islamic identity, are anxious to maintain their American roots. Thus, differences between the American-born Muslims and those who were raised overseas will continue to be a source of strain, each group fervently believing that their world view is ultimately better for the future of the community. . . .

A great number of second- and third-generation Muslim women are alienated by attempts at reform. In some cases they feel that those Muslim men who insist on eliminating the social function of the mosque are not being true Muslims. They point to the equal status and role of women at the time of the Prophet. Efforts to keep them out of the "male-space" are seen as reactionary and old-fashioned.[7] They point to the loss of a substantial number of third- and fourth-generation young people to Christianity (through intermarriage) or to secular society as a reaction to unnecessary strictures. These strictures, they believe, are un-Islamic, but, as one second-generation mother said, "are designed by men for the glory of men."

Finally, Muslims have experienced a considerable amount of prejudice in the United States. In addition to general public ignorance about the teachings of Islam, there is an accumulated heritage of mistrust that has lingered since the Crusades. . . .

Non-westernized new immigrants have formerly func-

7. Men and women pray in separate spaces in mosques. Sometimes women pray in a balcony or behind a curtained-off section. How much room is designated for women varies.

tioned as conservative agents, maintaining the validity of the home culture and restraining others from innovative changes. The number of future immigrants, as well as the nature of their commitment to Islam, will no doubt influence the shape Islam will take in the United States. Should a substantial number immigrate from among those committed to national rather than Muslim identity, as in the most recent immigration from Iran, and should they be willing to subsidize the Islamic organizations, a shift to a less normative Islam may eventually appear.

A Daughter of Yemeni Immigrants

Shams Alwujude

The author of this selection was obtaining an undergraduate degree in Dearborn, Michigan, when she wrote this memoir about growing up as the daughter of Yemeni immigrants. She published her essay under the pseudonym of Shams Alwujude to protect the privacy of family members. With economic prospects dim in rural Yemen, Alwujude's father first sought work in the wealthy gulf states of the Arabian Peninsula before coming to America. He then returned to bring most of his family with him to the south end of Dearborn, home to one of America's largest Arab American populations. Life was extremely difficult for this first generation of immigrants. Yet, as Alwujude describes in her essay, the second generation—"the children of America"—also faced many hardships. Alwujude describes her struggle to hold fast to her identity as a Muslim woman while facing prejudice from Americans outside her community. At the same time she fought to resist pressures from within her community to conform to gender roles for women that she no longer found appropriate.

My parents grew up in the same village in Yemen. My father fell in love with my mother after watching her from a distance while she did her chores. He, being the handsomest young man in the village, married who he thought was the most beautiful girl. My soon-to-be mother moved into his family home and shortly thereafter they started a family.

My parents both came from peasant farming families. What food they had to eat came from what dairy products they could get from the cow they owned and from whatever crops they were able to harvest, if it rained and the crops grew. Because my parents had a difficult existence, my father had to leave the country to find a decent job. He worked for a while in the Persian Gulf island nation of Bahrain. Eventually, my father looked to America, the land of tremendous opportunity for those who seek it, where he had a cousin who worked at a factory and earned a decent living. This cousin was the man who helped my father find work in the United States, and the same man who would later convince my father not to allow my sister and me to immigrate to America with the family.

A Father's Journey to America

I sometimes think about the difficulties my father must have had when he decided to go to America—to leave a culture that was his own, the country where his ancestors were buried; to go to a new land with another language, a land where people dress, look, act, and believe differently than would a Yemeni farmer's son. The one thing that my father had in common with other Americans, he believed, was that he sought a better way of life, just as the earlier immigrants to America did. He felt that because it was a country founded by and made up of immigrants, he would only naturally blend in. . . .

He eventually got to the camp [where he picked grapes in California] where he lived and worked with other Yemenis and sent whatever money he earned to Yemen to support his growing family, his parents, and his siblings.

After working a while in America my father would travel back to Yemen to be with his family, and then he would go back to America to work. When I was born my father was in Yemen. . . .

A Sister Left Behind

My family immigrated to the Southend of Dearborn in the summer of 1972, a year after I was born. My father had a well-paying job working on the assembly line in the Ford Rouge Plant and was able to have us brought close to him. We rented a flat in a house owned by my father's cousin, the same man who always insisted that females should not immigrate to America. In fact, when we did finally come here so that we could live with my father, we left my sister behind. We immigrated to the United States without her. My father also wanted to leave me behind, but my mother would not allow it because I was only a baby.

My sister was eight years old when she was left behind. She was told that we would be back in a year or two and that she should take care of our grandparents until we got back. This was my father and his cousin's idea. They felt that girls should not be raised in the United States, that they were better off in the old country where they could be protected from any and all evils that might be found in the new country's foreign culture and ideas. My mother, when leaving my sister behind, honestly thought that we would be going back to Yemen. Life's circumstances, such as my father losing his job, led to our not being able to go back to Yemen. My mother remained separated from my sister for nine agonizingly long years. It had not been her choice to leave her.

Facing Prejudice Outside the Arab Community

My earliest memory of being aware of my identity is when I was five years old. We had moved to a neighborhood in Detroit that year, out of the safety of the Arab culture of the Southend. We moved into a neighborhood where we were one of only two Arab families. One of our next door neighbors did not appreciate that we had bought the house next to theirs. They made sure to let us know this at every opportunity.

One day, when I was five, I was sitting on the front sidewalk playing with some rocks—an innocent child not knowing what kind of hatred lurked in the world. The teenage girl who lived next door approached me and started calling me a camel jockey. Not only did she call me this, she started cheering, like a cheerleader does, about my being a camel jockey. The cheer she used was a popular cheer called "Firecracker." For the word "firecracker," she substituted the words "camel jockey." I remember sitting on the sidewalk staring at her in awe, not really understanding what she was talking about, but realizing that when she said "camel jockey," she was saying it at me and that it was a very negative word. I also remember sensing her disdain when she looked at me. . . .

Sometimes I feel that I might be discriminated against because I dress differently than the average American and that it threatens people. But when I was five, and I was sitting on the sidewalk being called a camel jockey, I did not dress differently than any other five-year-old kid in this country. So I, with my assimilated clothing and English-speaking capabilities, had not warranted my neighbors' angry looks.

After my neighbor finished her camel jockey cheer . . . I ran into my house to find my mother. I knew that I was not this bad "camel jockey" word, so I asked my mother what I was. She said that I was an Arab. That sounded right to me. I told my mother what that girl had said. My mother, not knowing how to speak any English, and also being afraid of those people, told me to stay in the house and play. I was not even allowed to go to kindergarten that year because my mother was worried that something might happen to me. I remember vividly that one of the males who was not appreciative of our ethnicity once threatened me, a five year old, with a switchblade. It was very soon after this that we moved back to the Southend of Dearborn. The night after we moved, the house in Detroit was burned down. My parents suspected the neighbors did it.

My family bought a home in the Southend because many of the people there had the same culture we did. My mother had new neighbors that she could communicate with. We felt embraced by other Arab families who had the same concerns that we did about being in a different culture. Like us, they wanted to be a part of it, but they did not want to give up their own identities. Since this is a free country, there was always the sense that if we did not want to give up some of our traditional Yemeni customs, we did not have to. So my parents sent us into the schools, and I got to go to school because my mother felt it was safe.

Living in Two Cultures

The older my brothers and I got, the more we became aware of our dual cultures. One culture was that of television, which, more importantly, we also found in our school. The other culture was that of our home.

When we were in school six to seven hours a day, we were exposed to a curriculum that catered to Christians of European descent. I remember how absurd it was when we Arab Muslim children would sing in the Christmas concert that was done every year (the school was made up of mostly Muslim Arab children) and that the teachers would say "Merry Christmas" to us when we did not even celebrate the holiday. The teachers didn't even ask us if we celebrated it or not. I wondered if they assumed that we did or if they did not care whether we did. Needless to say, it was a very awkward situation where two cultures met and assumed not to notice the differences they had.

After the long days with our teachers who were all, as I recall, ethnically European Christian people, the same kind of people who belonged to the culture that we watched on TV, we went back home. As soon as we walked over the threshold into our house, we walked into Yemen. We would immediately be met by the mother whom we spoke to in Arabic. We would be in a home decorated with pictures of Muslim holy places and handwoven *debegs* used to serve Yemeni breads. . . .

My mother would also remind us of our religion when prayer time came (five times a day). She would do her ritual washing before the obligatory prayer, then spread the neatly folded prayer rug toward Mecca and start praying where we could see her.

Free to Choose Who I Am in America

In this Yemeni world, I had a certain role to play based on my gender. . . . As I got older, my mother started asking me to wear the *hijab*, the head scarf that Muslim women wear. When I started wearing it, it was easy since all of the Yemeni women I knew wore it. When I asked what it was about, my mother said that we wear it because we are Muslims, that it is part of our religion. That was as good an explanation as I needed at the time. Later in my life when I was faced with a crisis and was looking for help from God, I had a profound religious experience during which I realized the significance of wearing the *hijab*. I understood my identity as a Muslim woman, and that the *hijab* identified me as one of "the believing women" the Holy Quran talks about. I realized that my ethnic heritage is significant and legitimate and cannot be ignored. It is significant to the extent that those who hate Muslims hate me because I am one, even though they have never met me. I knew and loved who I was historically and became able to see how beautiful people of other cultures were. My recognition of my Yemeni history helps me to know which way I should be heading in my life. I choose to dress like a Muslim so that I may honor my religious beliefs and my identity. I wear my *hijab* and also my *jilbab* (a long robelike dress) in order to feel sacred and in touch with God.

I learned to believe in God and that He would be the only One that I would submit to. In so believing, I had embraced my cultural and ethnic heritage and rejected the Western idea that the less a woman wears the freer she is. I had found true freedom when I found God, and when I found Him I was fully dressed—there is absolutely no greater freedom that can be known (and people who have known God will attest to this) than the freedom one knows when one submits to God and is encompassed by Him. I felt, at the same time, that because I lived in a free country and the Bill of Rights guaranteed my religious freedom, that I was blessed to even make such a decision. I felt that I must be the ideal American. I am a Muslim Yemeni woman who espouses her identity wholeheartedly, but who also cherishes the ideals of freedom. By my very existence in this country, I prove that this is truly a free country because I can be who I am, not who the conformists want me to be. If I am made to submit by assimilation into the dominant culture, then how could this country be called "free"? Certainly many of my beliefs are Muslim, but I also sincerely believe in the ideals that this country was founded on, in the Constitution and in the Bill of Rights, and I do consider myself an American who would fight for the cause of freedom.

When I was a girl, like all other Muslim girls in this world, living in free countries or not, I received proposals of marriage. I remember the first time that I knew someone was proposing to my family. I was about twelve years old. I walked into the house after I had been playing outside. I don't remember why I went inside, but I found my mother on the telephone talking about me. She was saying things like "Yes, I understand, but she is too young"; "I know your family, you are very well respected, you come from an excellent family." My jaw dropped when I heard her say these things. I was petrified. I interrupted her, saying that I was only a child, that I could not get married yet, I had to go to junior high. After my mother finished talking on the phone, she explained to me that it was a man from Ohio who wanted me to become engaged to his son, and that he had no intention of my marrying him right away. My mother kindly said no to him, that I was too young.

A year later, however, my mother gave me a proposal of her own. She had gone to Yemen that year and after she came back, she showed me a picture of her nephew and said that he wanted to be engaged to me. She said that I would not have to marry him until I finished high school. I agreed to the engagement mostly because it meant that I was "taken," it was a guarantee that I could finish high school without worrying about marriage proposals. At age thirteen, I became engaged to my eighteen-year-old cousin whom I had never met or spoken to. We were engaged for four years. When I was seventeen, his mother died after giving birth to one too many babies. Because my fiancé was the oldest son and his mother had left behind a house full of children who needed someone to take care of them, he and his father looked to me to fill her role, but I had other plans. I had not finished high school as was the agreement, and besides that, at this point in my life I did not look at marrying a cousin as something that I wanted to do. Neither was I capable of going to Yemen and instantly becoming the mother of a house full of children or becoming a wife. We broke off the engagement, which then opened the door for others to propose.

Getting Married and Divorced

Many proposals came. Some were from cousins who wanted to marry me so that I might bring them into the country; others were just from young men who wanted to get married to start a family. I eventually accepted a proposal and got married when I was twenty years old, in 1991. At the time, I was considered an older bride. Most of the weddings then had brides who were still teenagers. I had graduated high school, which was very important to me. I had known girls who were married at young ages and consequently stopped attending school because they had started families. I did not want to do that. I knew that it was important for me to get an education. Marriage could wait, at least until I finished high school.

I remember when I first heard of the man I would later marry. I was preparing my sister's new house for my high school graduation party. My sister's husband told me that there was a man who was interested in marrying me and asked me if I would marry the man. I looked at my brother-in-law wanting to say, "Are you crazy?!" like I always wanted to say to him, but I tried to keep calm and asked him to tell me what the man's name was. He told me and then asked me again if I would marry him. I again kept calm and asked him to tell me more about this man. He said that he drove a taxicab in Detroit and that he also lived there. This information did not satisfy me. I could not make a decision to marry or not, so I asked my brother-in-law to find out more about him.

Eventually, this man who wanted to propose marriage paid a visit to our house and proposed in person. He did not propose to me, he proposed to my family.[1] My family did not see any reason not to like him. After an investigation into his family and their roots, and his reputation, he was deemed an acceptable marriage partner. After he passed my family's tests, it was up to me to decide whether

1. In traditional Arab culture both Muslim and Christian families believed that a marriage was a marriage not just of individuals, but of families. Parents expected to arrange the marriage or to be asked for their approval.

I would marry him or not. I agreed to marry him. I agreed to the marriage for several reasons. I was out of high school. I was tired of living at home and could not leave home unless I got married. I thought that marriage and family life would be much more fulfilling than going to college. . . .

The wedding night came and went. Nine months after we were married, our son was born. I had never felt such blessing and love than when he was born. God had smiled down upon me and gave me this child who would be a light in my life. My marriage was not a marriage. I tried to "make it work" but it never did. My husband and I separated, then eventually divorced. Afterward, I decided to go back to school so that I could earn a degree that I could use to get a decent, secure job. I found myself having to support myself and my child; I could no longer look to a man to support me.

Children of America

Even though I was engaged and married in a very Yemeni way, I took to the marriage some beliefs that were American in influence, which might have contributed to my eventual divorce. Because I grew up in America, even though where I grew up was made up of ethnic immigrants, I was influenced by American ideas that belonged to mainstream American culture. I am reminded of this American influence by Yemeni people who call their children who grow up in America, *'eyal imreeka*, which means "children of America."

Older Yemeni women sometimes compare themselves and their former difficult lives in Yemen with the "easy" lives that their daughters have in this country. This makes our existence even more difficult because we do not have it easy. It is not easy to be an identifiable ethnic immigrant. It is not easy to be a Muslim woman who wants to wear the *hijab* and has to deal with people who think of her as being oppressed by it—a piece of fabric. These people never really understand that what truly oppresses Muslim women is that which oppresses all women. It is also not easy to be a Muslim Arab immigrant in this country, because America occasionally makes immigrants feel unwelcome. Besides the pressures of mainstream American culture, 'eyal imreeka are pressured by the guilt sometimes put on them by their elders, who had to live a more difficult existence—so difficult an existence that one might lose his mind—as happened to my father.

The Sacrifices of an Immigrant Father

I have not mentioned my father very much in my story. In the fall of 1987, when I was sixteen years old, my father had a nervous breakdown. He had been having trouble finding work after he was laid off from Ford Motor Company, and he had other problems that my parents were excellent at keeping away from us children. We did not expect what was about to happen to us. Our father went insane before our very eyes. I had never felt so absolutely devastated. I felt like the world was pulled from under my feet. All that I had believed in was an illusion. The strongest most influential man in my life had instantly disappeared and was replaced by a man who inhabits his body and mumbles to himself.

I remember hiding in my room not wanting to look when the police handcuffed him and took him away. He was sent to a hospital for mental patients in Northville, Michigan. He had become suddenly violent toward my mother. He hallucinated that she was plotting against him with some of our family friends. I remember coming home from school and seeing my mother looking very distraught. My father had never laid a hand on her before. They were a very happy couple who, when in front of us, would often flirt and play with each other. I remember that when my mother was feeling ill, my father would have no problem cooking for us and cleaning the house. My mother often told me stories of how, after arriving from America to visit the family in Yemen, my father would hide presents for her so that his mother and sisters would not know and would not be jealous. He made sure that she wore the latest Yemeni fashions and that she had everything that she wanted.

Oftentimes I think about how my father struggled, how his life was totally devoted to us. He lived his whole life to bring his children to freedom and opportunity. He didn't even have the chance to get an education. From a very early age, before he was a teenager, he had to leave the village to find work because he was the oldest son and was therefore obligated to support his parents and siblings, who stayed on the farm. As soon as he became older, but was still a teenager, he married my mother and started a family, as was the custom. My mother brags that we were the first family in the village to wear shoes. My father worked abroad and sent enough money so we could buy them. The demands of his growing family kept him working very hard to provide the necessities of life. When he wasn't able to provide for us anymore, due to forces beyond his control, he slipped away from the rational world into a dreamworld of his own.

I feel that it is absolutely necessary for me to succeed in my life in this country. If I don't, all my parents did would have been in vain, even though they had the intention of seeing my brothers succeeding in this country, while all I was supposed to do was get married. Times change, and then so do expectations. God willing, I will remind my son of our story when he is a grown man. It's a shame that people forget what immigrants go through to try to grow roots in a new land. I hope my son will not forget what we went through and that he will use our story as fuel to drive him so that he might fulfill the hopes of his immigrant parents.

CHAPTER 3

A Marginalized Minority

COMING TO AMERICA

Anti-Arab Hate and Discrimination

Carol Khawly, Kareem Shora, and Hussein Ibish

The American-Arab Anti-Discrimination Committee (ADC) was founded in 1980 by former U.S. senator James Abourezk as a way to fight a rising tide of anti-Arab hate crimes. Hate crimes against Arab Americans often erupted in the United States following turmoil in the Middle East or terrorist acts committed in many places around the world. Through its efforts to track and report hate crimes, the ADC has helped demonstrate the need for the U.S. government to take action to stem the tide of anti-Arab hate crimes.

Since its founding, the ADC has regularly issued reports documenting acts of hate and discrimination committed against Arab Americans. This selection is taken from the *1998–2000 Report on Hate Crimes and Discrimination Against Arab Americans*. The authors detail a variety of hate crimes and discriminatory acts, such as physical assaults and employment discrimination. The following sections of the report were written by Carol Khawly, legal adviser to the ADC; Kareem Shora, legal attorney for the ADC; and Hussein Ibish, communications director of the ADC and a regular contributor to the *Los Angeles Times*.

Like many minority groups in the United States, Arab Americans often suffer discrimination and denial of their basic rights. In addition to dealing with discrimination and civil rights abuses at the hands of private entities and fel-

Carol Khawly, Kareem Shora, and Hussein Ibish, "Legal Issues," *1998–2000 Report on Hate Crimes and Discrimination Against Arab Americans*. Washington, DC: ADC Research Institute, 2001. Copyright © 2001 by ADC Research Institute. Reproduced by permission of the American-Arab Anti-Discrimination Committee (ADC).

low citizens, Arab Americans have increasingly faced a set of discriminatory policies from the federal government, including the use of airport profiling and secret evidence in deportation cases. As a result, ADC's Legal Department on a daily basis deals with cases involving workplaces, service industries, and schools, as well as federal and state agencies. Discriminatory policies by government agencies reinforce anti-Arab attitudes and encourage bigotry against the Arab-American community. Such policies and practices reflect and reinforce rampant anti-Arab stereotypes in the mass media . . . contributing to a climate in which hate crimes and discrimination against Arab Americans are all too common.

Tracking Hate Crimes and Discrimination

ADC's Legal Department each week receives numerous phone calls, e-mail messages, and letters reporting discrimination in areas of employment, education, housing, police misconduct, immigration rights, and other concerns. . . . Thirty-five percent of the cases received from 1998–2000 were employment discrimination cases and another thirty-five percent were cases involving other forms of institutionalized discrimination, such as immigration and airline passenger profiling. Twenty-two percent of the reported cases received were hate crimes.

Many of those who contact our office are not familiar with the laws that safeguard their rights in the United States, particularly federal laws prohibiting discrimination based on national origin, race, religion, sex, and disability. One of the main missions of ADC is to provide legal advice and counseling to those who have reason to feel that they have been subjected to illegal discrimination, and to refer those with actionable cases to other attorneys. ADC's Legal Department is also mandated to track the pattern of discrimination and hate crimes directed against the Arab-

American community, and that work is reflected in this section of the Report.

Physical and Psychological Attacks

Personal attacks of both the physical and psychological kind on Arabs and Arab Americans in the United States are part of the regular pattern of hate crimes that many in the community have been forced to endure.

Physical attacks, although less common than their psychological counterparts, include such criminal offenses as battery and vandalism. Often such attacks are categorized as felonies under criminal law. A majority of these crimes are covered under the laws of the various states as opposed to federal statutes. However, a very significant federal penalty for such crimes comes into play if a crime is deemed to be a "hate crime" committed with the intent of attacking someone based, in whole or in part, on their religion, race, ethnicity, and/or national origin. Although there are no official government statistics on such crimes committed specifically against Arab Americans due to the lack of federal recognition of Arab Americans as a minority group, ADC routinely receives complaints of such attacks.

Psychological attacks, better known under criminal law as assault and/or threats with the intent to commit a crime, are the more common type of personal attacks faced by Arab Americans. These crimes often go unreported due to the perceived insignificance of their impact on the victim. Although not all derogatory comments made against the national origin and/or religion of an individual are included as crimes under the various criminal statutes, these offenses often stem from the widely held negative stereotypes of Arabs in American popular culture. It is important to note that a comment, no matter how derogatory, does not constitute a crime and is indeed protected as free speech under the First Amendment of the United States

Constitution. The only manner in which a derogatory comment may be viewed as a crime is if the comment incorporates, either in words or in action, what is defined under criminal statutes as "hate speech." Speech may be prosecuted as a crime under "hate speech" statutes if it directly incites physical violence, in any form, against its intended victim or the group to which the intended victim belongs. Legal standards for "hate speech" statutes and their enforcement vary significantly depending on the jurisdiction.

The victim of these attacks, whether physical or psychological, may pursue remedy in civil action against the offender independently of any criminal charges. . . .

Physical Attacks

[Among ten cases of physical attacks listed in the report are the following three:]

December 1997—Washington, DC: A Muslim crescent-and-star was displayed alongside the national Christmas tree and Jewish menorah on the Ellipse in front of the White House to signify the holy month of Ramadan. Shortly after its unveiling, the artist who built the 10-foot-tall wooden structure discovered the star torn from the crescent, painted with a red swastika, and thrown near a garbage can a few hundred feet away. The Moroccan-born artist, who was taking a friend to look at the Muslim symbol when he made the discovery, alerted the U.S. Park authorities who investigated the incident as a hate crime. In response to calls from Arab-American and Muslim groups to condemn the act of vandalism, President Clinton issued a statement denouncing the desecration as "the embodiment of intolerance that strikes at the heart of what it means to be an American.". . .

February 1999—Montgomery County, MD: David Leonard Rikon was charged with hate violence and malicious destruction of property for his part in harassing long-time ADC educational activist Samira Hussein and her family. The Husseins' ordeal began during the Gulf War [of 1991].[1] Throughout this period, the Hussein family reported five acts of vandalism to the police. Among these acts were: a rock thrown across the patio shattering a glass door; the doors to the family car being glued shut; and trash strewn all over the lawn. In September of 1997, a swastika and the word "pig" were etched on the hood of Hussein's car, the seats were slashed, and the tires punctured. Leonard Rikon, a neighbor of the Husseins, was found guilty and convicted of hate violence and malicious destruction of property on March 10, 1999.

March 2001—Tucson, AZ: A Palestinian family, who had just moved in to a Tucson, Arizona, neighborhood, had their property vandalized when someone threw eggs all over their front yard. When the mother called the police, she was told that it was just "teenage stuff" and that it should not be taken seriously. Two weeks later, someone once again threw eggs all over the front yard. This time, the vandals left a box full of hate messages and a knife covered in ketchup. One of the messages called the daughter a "rock thrower" and a "bitch." The police concluded that this was a hate crime and collected all the items as evidence. This event left the entire family in fear and the mother afraid of letting her children attend school the following week, fearing that they could he harmed. . . .

Employment Discrimination

Employment discrimination on many grounds is illegal under state and federal laws. The primary federal law prohibiting discrimination is incorporated in Title VII of the Civil Rights Act of 1964. Federal law prohibits employment discrimination based on any of eight categories: race,

1. In the Gulf War of 1991 the United States and its allies repulsed the Iraqi invasion of Kuwait.

religion, color, age, sex, disability, citizenship status and national origin. It is also illegal for an employer to penalize an employee for exercising his or her right to oppose and report any of these forms of discrimination. The fact that an employee has complained or filed a charge of discrimination, or has participated in a discrimination investigation or proceeding as a complainant or witness, cannot be held against the employee. . . . State law and local ordinances may also prohibit discrimination based on marital status, occupation, sexual orientation, political opinion and personal appearance. ADC's Legal Department personnel are available to provide more details on the complaint process. The ADC Research Institute has also published a number of pamphlets and guides which explain your rights.

ADC receives an average of 25 complaints per week that allege employment discrimination. Most of ADC's employment discrimination complaints are based on national origin and religion. For example, one Arab employee was asked to change the name on his name tag from Mohammed to "Al" to increase sales. Ethnic slurs and other physical conduct relating to an individual's national origin also constitute harassment when it has the purpose or effect of creating a "hostile work environment" such as unreasonably interfering with an individual's work performance. Muslim women who wear the *hijab* (a head scarf covering the hair) are particularly vulnerable to job discrimination because their religious practice makes them conspicuous. In recent years, the number of discrimination complaints by Muslim women who wear the *hijab* have increased dramatically. For example, women who decide to start wearing the *hijab* after being employed are often forced to choose between removing it and being dismissed. Therefore, it is important for all individuals to report incidents of harassment to the employer in a timely manner, requesting an employee manual and being aware of the employer's reporting procedures.

Approximately 35% of all legal complaints received by ADC annually relate to the hostile work environment employees experience during their work or the employer's lack of accommodation for religious practices. . . .

Employment Discrimination Case Summaries

[Among twenty-five cases of employment discrimination listed in the report are the following two:]

October 1998—Washington, DC: A complaint was filed with the EEOC [U.S. Equal Employment Opportunity Commission] against a Chicago-based international law firm for allegedly discriminating against a female employee who was Muslim. The employee wore a *hijab* . . . on the job. The firm allegedly complained to the employee about the scarf and then dismissed her after learning that she would not remove the hijab. The firm stated that the incident was "an honest human mistake" made by an employer unfamiliar with Muslim religious practices. As a result of an EEOC investigation of the complaint, the employee was offered an apology and compensation for lost salary. . . .

December 1999—Oakland, MI: A jury awarded a sizable monetary remedy to Ahmad Abu-Aziz, a former United Airlines employee, in a case of extreme ethnic discrimination. At trial, Abu-Aziz's attorney proved to the court that his client was the victim of harassment and was fired on the basis of false accusations of misconduct stemming from his complaints of discrimination. For four months, Abu-Aziz worked at Oakland International Airport cleaning airplane interiors during which time he complained of harassment to his superiors. Although the ridicule soon ended, he was terminated six weeks after his initial complaint due to accusations by his coworkers that he was stealing alcohol and drinking on the job. The United Airlines manager responsible for firing Abu-Aziz reportedly knew the accusations were false but used them as a justification for the dismissal. During the course of the trial, the court learned of the constant humiliation and harassment experienced by Abu-Aziz at United Airlines. When he first met his supervisor at United Airlines, the official allegedly made fun of Abu-Aziz's name and singled him out for the largely undesired and dirty assignment of cleaning out all the airplane lavatories, not as is normally done with a brush, but with his bare hands. Furthermore, a flight attendant supposedly told him in front of his co-workers that he "looked like a terrorist.". . .

Institutionalized Discrimination

Institutionalized discrimination includes racial or ethnic bias which occurs within a specific system, procedure or organization. Most instances of institutionalized discrimination faced by Arab Americans come from agencies of the federal government, such as FAA-mandated profiling of airline passengers and INS use of secret evidence and mandatory detention (indefinite detention) in deportation cases. These instances of official, institutionalized discrimination are among the most troubling that Arab-Americans face.

After the crash of TWA Flight 800 in 1996, which was subsequently determined to be a 'mechanical failure,' President Clinton appointed Vice-President Gore to chair a White House Commission on Aviation Safety and Security. The Commission's recommendations included . . . that the FAA mandate an automated passenger profiling system which later became known as CAPPS (Computer-Assisted Passenger Pre-Screening System). CAPPS . . . went into effect in January 1998. Its use is mandatory in all US airports and by all US airlines operating overseas.

Profiling is a system that compares an individual with an officially compiled abstract of characteristics thought typical of someone who might be a threat to airline safety. If there is a significant correlation, the person will be subject to greater scrutiny.

The profiling software runs on an airline's reservation system and scores passengers based on a set of weighted criteria. Of the forty or so pieces of data, only a few are known. The rest are confidential. The known criteria include a passenger's starting point, destination, time of travel, method of payment, past criminal record, and whether the passenger's ticket is one-way or round trip. Testimony before a House Transportation Subcommittee revealed that for each criterion, a passenger receives a positive or negative value. If the total score is below a certain cutoff, that individual is selected for additional security which may include intense questioning and a physical item-by-item baggage search, often in a humiliating and very public context.

Although the FAA claims that profiling is in no way discriminatory, the disproportionate number of complaints made by Arab Americans indicates that profiling either targets Arab Americans or, at the very least, is having a disparate impact on them. At the same time, the FAA has not been able to point to a single instance in which profiling has led to the identification of any person posing an actual threat to airport or aircraft security. . . .

In conjunction with many other civil rights organizations, ADC opposes profiling in general. It is our belief that profiling, even under the best circumstances, provides an opportunity for the prejudices and stereotypes held by law enforcement and other officials to be expressed through discriminatory application of profiles. At worst, they are simply a recipe for bigoted behavior. ADC supports all efforts in Congress and executive agencies to track, limit and eliminate all uses of profiling in American law enforcement.

ADC has received hundreds of complaints from Arab and Arab-American airline passengers of discrimination at airports. This report contains only a small sample of the complaints we received about airline passenger harassment at airports in a period spanning from July 1998 to March 2001. . . .

Airline Passenger Profiling Case Summaries

[Among twenty profiling cases listed in the report are the following two:]

American Airlines

December 1998—Dulles International Airport, VA: An Arab man entered the American Airlines terminal with his mother to go to Aruba via Miami for a medical conference. The representative from American Airlines approached the traveler and took his passport and plane ticket. He then asked him to wait, without giving any explanation. The traveler waited for fifteen minutes while other passengers were being processed. He asked to speak to the supervisor who explained to him that he would not have sufficient time to board his flight. The traveler noticed that other passengers standing in line behind him, some of whom were foreign nationals, continued to be processed and were allowed to board the flight. He was re-routed to a different airport and had to travel to Aruba via New York through San Juan. As a result, the Arab man missed the first day of his medical conference. Subsequently, during a phone interview, the American Airlines supervisor informed him that the reason for this incident was his national origin. . . .

United Airlines

July 1999—Frankfurt International Airport, Germany: An Arab-American family was traveling from Lebanon to Washington via Frankfurt when they were asked several questions about carrying illegal weapons while trying to get their boarding passes. After having denied knowledge of any weapons, they were told to step aside. They were then led to an underground room where two employees searched all four pieces of luggage, including three carry-on pieces, claiming it was a "policy procedure." Despite this claim, there were no other passengers being searched. After expressing continued confusion, the family was told that if they wanted to complain they should take it up with the US government and the FAA. Finally, a supervisor admitted that they were being detained because they came from Lebanon. After all the passengers had boarded, security escorted the family to the waiting plane which departed an hour late. As a result, the family missed their connecting flight in Washington, where they were forced to spend the night.

Combating Anti-Arab Stereotyping

Marvin Wingfield and Bushra Karaman

Anti-Arab stereotypes, such as depictions of Arabs as war-like, lustful heathens, have been embedded in Western culture for nearly eight centuries. In more recent times Arabs and Arab Americans have been vilified in a variety of contemporary media aimed at children, including cartoons, video games, and movies. Educators have long been aware that children readily absorb these stereotypes. Not only does this absorption help breed intolerance among children of the dominant culture, it also damages the self-image and pride of Arab American children. In this selection Marvin Wingfield and Bushra Karaman argue that classroom teachers who are aware of the negative stereotyping of African Americans, Hispanics, Jews, and other ethnic groups are often unaware of the anti-Arab biases in school texts and in the media. They recommend that schools regularly teach about the historic achievements of Arab civilizations and give the study of Arabic culture and language greater prominence in American schools. Wingfield is the director of education and outreach at the American-Arab Anti-Discrimination Committee. Karaman is a Palestinian American teacher and resource consultant in Dearborn, Michigan.

When American children hear the word "Arab", what is the first thing that comes to mind? Perhaps the imagery of Disney's Arabian Nights' fantasy film *Aladdin*, a film which has been immensely popular in theaters and on

Marvin Wingfield and Bushra Karaman, "Arab Stereotypes and American Educators," *Social Studies and the Young Learner*, March/April 1995, pp. 7–10. Copyright © 1995 by the American-Arab Anti-Discrimination Committee (ADC). Reproduced by permission.

video and is sometimes shown in school classrooms.

Yet Arab Americans have problems with this film. Although in many ways it is charming, artistically impressive, and one of the few American films to feature an Arab hero or heroine, a closer look reveals some disturbing features.

The film's light-skinned lead characters, Aladdin and Jasmine, have Anglicized features and Anglo-American accents. This is in contrast to the other characters who are dark-skinned, swarthy and villainous—cruel palace guards or greedy merchants with Arabic accents and grotesque facial features.

The film's opening song sets the tone;

Oh, I come from a land,
From a faraway place
Where the caravan camels roam.
Where they cut off your ear
If they don't like your face.
It's barbaric, but hey, it's home.

Thus the film immediately characterizes the Arab world as alien, exotic, and "other." Arab Americans see this film as perpetuating the tired stereotype of the Arab world as a place of deserts and camels, of arbitrary cruelty and barbarism.

Therefore, Arab Americans raised a cry of protest regarding *Aladdin*. The American-Arab Anti-Discrimination Committee (ADC) challenged Disney and persuaded the studio to change a phrase in the lyrics for the video version of the film to say: "It's flat and immense, and the heat is intense. It's barbaric, but hey, it's home." While this is an improvement, problems remain.

ADC President Candace Lightner, founder of Mothers Against Drunk Driving, comments, "I was angry and embarrassed when I listened to the *Aladdin* lyrics while watching the movie. I could only hope that the audience was not paying close attention and would not take home with them a poor image of the Arab world." She adds, "I only wish Disney had consulted us first before they developed a movie, reaching millions of people, based on our culture. This is why there is an ADC." Grassroots protest has also been successful in combatting the troubling elements of this film. In Illinois, a 10-year-old Arab American girl persuaded a music teacher leading the school chorus to discard the offensive *Aladdin* lyrics—although she had to explain three times why the lyrics were offensive before the teacher "got it."

Arabs in Popular Culture

Disney is by no means the only offender. Popular culture aimed at children is replete with negative images of Arab women as belly dancers and harem girls, and Arab men as violent terrorists, oil "sheiks," and marauding tribesmen who kidnap blond Western women.

Arabs are frequently cast as villains on Saturday morning TV cartoons, Fox Children Network's *Batman*, for example. This cartoon portrayed fanatic, dark-complexioned Arabs armed with sabers and rifles as allies of an "alien" plotting to take over the Earth.

[In the early 1990s] Spencer Gift stores sold "Arab" Halloween masks with grotesque physical features, along with their usual array of goblin, demon, and vampire masks. The chain stocked no other ethnic masks.

Comic books frequently have Arab villains as a gratuitous element in their story line: Tarzan battles with an Arab chieftain who kidnaps Jane, Superman foils Arab terrorists hijacking a U.S. nuclear carrier, and the Fantastic Four combat a hideous oil sheik supervillain. But, as Lebanese American media analyst Jack Shaheen comments, "There is never an Arab hero for kids to cheer."

Negative portraits of Arabs are found in numerous popular films, such as *True Lies, Back to the Future,* and *Raiders of the Lost Ark.*

Computer games often feature cartoon Arab villains in which children rack up high scores and win games by killing Arabs.

Ethnic stereotypes are especially harmful in the absence of positive ethnic images. Shaheen observes that Arabs are "hardly ever seen as ordinary people, practicing law, driving taxis, singing lullabies or healing the sick."

Arab Stereotypes Among Educators

Popular films and television imprint young children with numerous negative images of Arabs, and American educators do not do enough to correct this bias. Many do not even perceive anti-Arab racism as a problem. Educators who have not yet been alerted to this issue and are unaware of the potential harm being done are themselves part of the problem.

Despite the multicultural philosophy that currently prevails in American education, ADC has found many teachers and the public at large not yet sufficiently sensitized to the problem of anti-Arab and anti-Muslim stereotyping. While multicultural articles, books, and curriculum teaching units may deal with the heritage of African American, Hispanic, Native American and Asian/Pacific American cultures—it is not unusual for them to ignore Arabs and the Middle East. One educator in Fairfax County, Virginia, commented that "The kids from the Middle East are the lost sheep in the school system. They fall through the cracks in our categories."

The Middle East Studies Association (MESA) and the Middle East Outreach Council (MEOC) have researched history and geography textbooks, finding "an overportrayal of deserts, camels and nomads" in the chapter on the Middle East. Even some well-intentioned teachers use the Bedouin image as somehow typifying "Arab culture." In fact, only about 2% of Arabs are traditional Bedouin, and today there are probably more Arab engineers and computer operators than desert dwellers.

American textbooks are often Eurocentric, while Arab points of view regarding such issues as the nationalization of resources or the Arab-Israeli conflict are presented inadequately or not at all. The MESA/MEOC study concluded that "The presentation of Islam is so problematic that it is perhaps time for educators at the college and university level to send a red alert to their colleagues at the precollegiate level. Crude errors and distortions abound." Some textbooks link Islam to violence and intolerance, ignoring its commonalities with Christianity and Judaism. While from a contemporary ecumenical or interfaith perspective, Yahweh, God the Father, and Allah (the generic word for God in Arabic) can be regarded as one God. Textbooks sometimes discuss Allah as if the word referred to an alien god remote from Jewish and Christian tradition.

Overt anti-Arab racism, while rare, does occur. ADC received a report that an Arab American student at a private school in Virginia was forbidden to go to her school prom with either a Black or a White date. "You are a foreigner," she was told by her teacher. "You must go with someone who has the same features."

Effects of Stereotyping on Arab American Children

What does it feel like for ArabAmerican children to grow up surrounded by a culture that does not recognize their ethnic identity in a positive way? They may find that the messages about the Arab world in school conflict with the values and traditions passed on at home. The images of Arabs which are conveyed in the classroom may have nothing in common with their relatives and experiences at home or their friends and relatives in the neighborhood, church/mosque, or elsewhere. They also find their peers to be influenced by negative and inaccurate images and preconceptions about the Arab heritage. Obviously these circumstances lead to hurtful experiences.

Dr. Shaheen remembers being taught in his Lebanese American home to be proud of his family's Arab heritage. But at school, he remembers teasing, taunts, and epithets: "camel jockeys," "desert higgers," "greasy Lebs."

Shaheen reports that his children were deeply upset when eight students in the annual Halloween parade at their school dressed up as "Arabs"—with accessories such as big noses, oil cans or money bags to complete the costume. Later, at the school's ethnic festival, "our children were hesitant to wear ethnic costumes," he said.

Others report similar incidents. Carol Haddad, a second-generation American of Lebanese and Syrian ancestry, describes her experience at age ten: "Each time I left the security of my family house, I experienced the oppression of being darker and different." Her family was stared at on the street, and Irish and German American children in their neighborhood mocked her family for "eating leaves" when they served grape leaves stuffed with spiced lamb and rice. During an argument, a boy in her neighborhood called her a "nigger."

An ADC staffer recalls that, when she was growing up, her class was taught about Jewish culture. "We danced the hora and I came home singing Jewish songs." But there was no equivalent teaching about Arab culture. "My father was so mad!"

Like other ethnics, Arab Americans frequently encounter negative stereotypes disguised in the form of "humor." When they object, they are told that the derogatory comments were "not meant to be taken seriously." Today there should be greater public awareness and acknowledgement that not taking the identity of others seriously is just another form of racism.

More dangerous were the numerous incidents of anti-Arab hostility during the Gulf war [of 1991] with Iraq, when schools and communities were swept by patriotic fervor. The flags, banners, yellow ribbons, patriotic songs, and speakers from the military undermined teachers' efforts to encourage critical thinking about news reports and official statements. There was little chance of understanding Arab society or the humanity of the Iraqi people. Arab American students often felt intimidated and silenced, although the presence of students of Arab origin in classes served to heighten teachers' sensitivity to the human dimension of the conflict.

In Dearborn, Michigan, a proposal was brought before the Wolverine A basketball conference to disband all sports competition for the year. Some schools did not want to play with the team from Fordson High School, where half of the students and most of the basketball team were Arabs. Students from Fordson were told, "Go back to Saudi Arabia. You're not wanted here." A bomb threat was reported at the school. Students also reported fights with students from other schools during the previous year.

Often as they mature, Arab American young people consciously reclaim their ethnic identity. Lisa Suhair Majaj, a Palestinian American doctoral student, at the University of Michigan, observed, "Once I claimed a past, spoke my history, told my name, the walls of incomprehension and hostility rose, brick by brick: un-funny ethnic jokes; jibes about terrorists and kalashnikovs, and about veiled women and camels; or worse, the awkward silences, the hasty shifts to other subjects. Searching for images of my Arab self in American culture I found only unrecognizable stereotypes. In the face of such incomprehension I could say nothing."

What effect does this stereotyping have on the increasing numbers of Arab American students in the U.S. schools?

What can classroom teachers do about these problems?

It is recognized that the more positive a student's self-concept, the higher is his or her achievement level. Teachers use various techniques to make students feel worthwhile and important. But when Arab students see negative and erroneous portrayals of Arabs in films and on television, they begin to feel inferior and ashamed, or perhaps belligerent and aggressive.

Students suffer as a result of this. And learning suffers. Caught in this spiral, Arab American students may begin to believe that they, as a people, are inferior. They may stop trying to do their best and become convinced that they can never amount to anything. For many it becomes a self-fulfilling prophecy. As educators, we must break this cycle, by finding ways to intervene effectively.

In Dearborn, Michigan,[1] the schools' bilingual programs use Arab language and literature to make students from homes in which Arabic is spoken feel more culturally comfortable. Special programs, however, are not enough. It is important for mainstream teachers to consciously rid themselves of negative and ill-informed media images of Arabs (and other ethnic groups). It is also important for them to learn about their students' histories and cultures and to be prepared to teach about them in their classes.

The historic achievements of Arab culture are rarely discussed in American schools or are perhaps limited to 6th and 10th grade world history courses. In the culturally sensitive classroom, there is no good reason why a historical and cultural dimension cannot be provided. For example, math teachers can explain the cultural origins or development of "Arabic numerals," the decimal system, geometry and *al-jabr* (algebra) in ancient Greece, India, and the medieval Arab world. Science teachers can present

1. Dearborn, Michigan, has one of the highest concentrations of Arab Americans in the country.

the history of astronomy from ancient Babylon, Hellenic culture, and medieval Arab civilization as the precursor of modern science. Music classes can teach about Arabic music. Home economics classes can teach about Arab cuisine and its cultural meanings.

The Arabic language, a major world language, is spoken by some 200 million people. The Middle East is a region of strategic political and economic importance for the United States. Yet, the Arabic language is taught in only a handful of U.S. schools. Even in Dearborn, where 30% of the students are Arab, Arabic is offered only in the high schools of East Dearborn attended by the Arab students. It is not offered in West Dearborn schools with a higher proportion of non-Arabs.

In schools with minority populations, teachers should make an effort to abandon political biases and build on student's personal histories and existing knowledge bases, rather than ignore them or minimize their importance. Dearborn schools have made an attempt to build on the existing strengths of the students, including their Arabic language skills. Only when educators regard Arab students as having a rich and living culture, separate and distinct from the popular media images, can we have a proud new Arab American generation.

Struggling to Gain a Foothold in American Politics

Suad Joseph

Because Arab Americans represent many nationalities and religious traditions, forging a unified voice in the political arena was not easy. According to Suad Joseph, this effort was accomplished only after the Arab-Israeli war of 1967 galvanized the Arab American community in the wake of anti-Arab backlash. By the mid-1980s Arab Americans had succeeded in founding several effective advocacy groups, among them the American-Arab Anti-Discrimination Committee, which is dedicated to fighting hate crimes and anti-Arab stereotyping; and the Arab American Institute, whose goal is to help Arab Americans win elected positions in government. Joseph documents the gradual willingness of American political candidates to accept the endorsements of Arab Americans and to listen to their viewpoints regarding the Arab-Israeli conflict. Despite this progress, Joseph is not sanguine about the community's success in winning political clout. She cites a wave of anti-Arab hate crimes following the 1991 Gulf War and the willingness of newscasters to jump to the ill-founded conclusion that Arab terrorists were behind the Oklahoma City bombing in 1995 as indications that Arab Americans have yet to attain full citizenship. For this reason she refers to them as a hyphenated group whose hyphen has yet to end with the closure "American." She therefore uses the term *Arab-* instead of *Arab-American*. Professor Joseph is a member of the anthropology department at the University of California at Davis.

Suad Joseph, "Against the Grain of the Nation—The Arab- ," *Arabs in America: Building a New Future*, edited by Michael W. Suleiman. Philadelphia, PA: Temple University Press, 1999. Copyright © 1999 by Temple University. All rights reserved. Reproduced by permission of Temple University Press.

How have Arabs responded to the [negative] depictions of their societies of origin and the glossing of these depictions onto them? Earlier generations of Arab immigrants generally did not identify as Arab. From the nineteenth to the mid-twentieth century, most Arabs in America were Christians from Lebanon or Syria. The U.S. census of that time tended to label them as Ottomans, Turks, Asians, or Syrians. Given the smallness of their numbers and their tendency to scatter across small towns and rural areas, rather than consolidate in numbers in urban areas, most assimilated into mainstream culture in their local areas, joining mainstream businesses and the religious and social institutions and identifying mainly in terms of their families and religious sects.

Arab American Advocacy Organizations

The 1967 Arab-Israeli war was a turning point.[1] The often indiscriminate attacks on and public displays of hatred for Arabs and Arabs- during and after the war galvanized Arabs- to organize in America to fend off discriminatory representations of themselves and their homelands. The Association of Arab-American University Graduates (AAUG), founded in 1967, was the first Arab- organization with political-scholarly goals. The National Association of Arab Americans (NAAA) was founded in 1972. Its goal was to act as a political lobby in Washington on behalf of Arab issues. The first organization to systematically focus on discrimination against Arabs in America was the American-Arab Anti-Discrimination Committee (ADC),

1. In 1967 Egypt closed the Red Sea to Israeli shipping, ordered the withdrawal of UN peace keeping forces on the Egyptian-Israeli border, and signed defense agreements with Syria, Jordan, and Iraq. Israel then launched a preemptive surprise attack, lasting only six days, during which it was once again victorious against the combined effort of several Arab countries. Afterward, Israel occupied more of the remaining territory set aside for a Palestinian state, including the West Bank of the Jordan River, the Gaza Strip, and the Palestinian sector of Jerusalem. This humiliating defeat still brings rancor to the Arab world.

founded in 1980 by former Senator James Abourezk. For nineteen years, ADC has compiled and disseminated data on discrimination, taken legal actions, and met with American media representatives (especially the notoriously anti-Arab Disney Productions) to educate and pressure them to change their representation of Arabs in the media. ADC made sources, materials, and speakers available to the school systems, worked against the blacklisting of Arab-intellectuals and political activists. ADC has been a milestone in political activism on behalf of creating a space for Arabs- as American citizens.

Perhaps the most interesting organization in terms of the argument of this study is the Arab American Institute (AAI), founded in 1985 by James Zogby, an experienced activist leader in ADC. The goal of AAI has been to increase the political participation of Arabs- in the American political process. AAI has worked to create Arab Republican and Arab Democratic clubs, to support Arabs- of both major parties running for office, and to elect Arabs- to the national conventions and local offices of both parties.

Presidential Candidates Reject Arab American Support

When AAI was founded, I was taken aback. AAUG and ADC had made sense to me, and I joined both when they were formed. As a progressive, it was difficult for me to accept that people whom I knew and accepted as progressives were willing to work for conservative candidates as AAI was willing to do. In retrospect and in the context of the argument I propose in this [article], I now see their moves as claims for full citizenship for Arabs- in America. The outline of this program for active citizenship is laid out by Helen Hatab Samhan in her analysis of the 1988 elections, in which she argues that Arab Americans were a constituency come of age.

Arabs- had not been politically effective, Samhan argues, because they were unable to identify as a single community or because candidates, particularly Democratic Party candidates, refused to be associated with them. George McGovern [who ran for president] in 1972 rejected the endorsement of a group of Arab-American academics. In 1976, Jimmy Carter accepted a Lebanese American Committee rather than an Arab- committee. In 1980, an Arab-support group for Jimmy Carter was dissolved. Ronald Reagan in 1980 also did not accept Arab- support committees but accepted Lebanese American and Syrian American support committees. In 1984 [presidential candidate] Walter Mondale returned the checks of a group of Arab-American businessmen who had met with him and supported his campaign with checks of $1,000 each. He later apologized and appointed [Arab Americans] Mary Rose Oakar (D–OH), Nick Rahall (D–WV), and George Mitchell (D–ME) to serve as liaisons to the Arab-American community.

Acquiring Political Clout

The first time in the political history of Arab-American citizenship in this country that specifically defined Arab-American support committees were accepted by any presidential candidates—Jesse Jackson and Ronald Reagan—was in 1984. Other firsts in 1984 were the appointments of Arab Americans in prominent roles in presidential campaigns. George Salem was chief of the Ethnic Voters Division of the Reagan campaign, and James Zogby served as vice-chair and liaison to the Arab-American community for Jackson's campaign. In that campaign, Arab Americans became the largest single constituent group organized by the Ethnic Voters Division of the Reagan-Bush campaign. For the first time, an identified Arab-American activist, James Zogby, took the podium of the Democratic Party's national convention to offer a nominating speech for a presidential candidate—Jesse Jackson. For those of us aware of the struggle to get there, it was an overwhelming moment.

For the 1988 elections, AAI made a national effort to organize Arab Americans as a coherent force in the elections. Eleven thousand people and fifteen national institutions signed its election planks, eleven states participated in focused local organizing work, town meetings were held to discuss the 1988 Issues Agenda for Arab Americans, and intense work was invested in educating Arab Americans on how to get elected as delegates to national conventions. In California, thirty-nine Arab-American Democrats ran for national delegate positions, and in Texas, more than 125 ran. James Zogby served as national co-chair of the Jesse Jackson campaign.

The 1988 election was a watershed in the efforts of Arab Americans to put issues of Middle Eastern policy, particularly Palestine, into the national debates, a watershed with many low points and achievements. . . . Arab-American Democrats worked with Jesse Jackson to put a resolution in the national platform supporting Palestinian statehood. The negotiations, defeats, and achievements of this experience were another watershed of experience as politically active full American citizens for Arab Americans. As a spokesman for the Israeli embassy put it, "The significance of this is not in the adoption or non-adoption of the Jackson Mideast plank, but in the issue being debated as a major issue by one of the great parties."

Perhaps even more interesting was the statement by Larry Cohler and Walter Ruby in the *Washington Jewish Week*, in an article entitled "The New Arab American Activists." Cohler and Ruby observed that "the style of the Arab Americans is distinctly American and acts as a powerful tonic against the stereotype many Americans have come to hold of this ethnic group." The implication of this article is that Arabs- were operating according to the rules of the strategizing, contractarian, possessive individualist, rational actors recognizable as free persons, as citizens. Samhan takes these actions and statements as evidence that Arab Americans had come of age as citizens in the body politic of this nation.

An Uncertain Future

I am less sanguine in interpreting these events, as the Gulf War only a short three years after the 1988 elections painfully demonstrated. The shameful demonizing of Arabs during that war terrorized those of us with any sense of identity with the Arab- community. General Norman Schwartzkopf, head of our military operations in the Gulf, in a nationally televised news briefing, asserted that the Iraqis "are not part of the same human race we are. I have to pray that it is true.". . .

The *Sacramento Bee* carried a story, reproduced in little of the national press, reporting that U.S. Representative Norman Mineta "pointed to a 1987 contingency plan the FBI and the Immigration and Naturalization Service drew up to detain Arab Americans at a camp in Oakdale, [Louisiana], in the event of war with certain Arab states. Mineta said that plan could still be initiated to 'round up' Arab-Americans." Around the country, Islamic mosques were broken into or bombed, shots were fired into the homes of known Arabs-, a taxi driver in Fort Worth, Texas, was attacked and killed, some Muslim schools and Islamic societies were vandalized, and hate calls were received by Arabs- throughout that period.

In more recent years, the response to the [1993] bombing of the World Trade Center in New York City added to the furor against Arabs, Muslims, and Middle Easterners. The immediate assumption by the major national media, fed by comments by Attorney General Janet Reno, after the bombing of the federal building in Oklahoma City in 1995, was that this was an act of Muslim, Arab, Middle Eastern terrorists. For days after the arrests of free, white, male, Anglo, right-wing militia members as suspects in the bombing, the media persisted in making the association of bombings with Muslims, Arabs, and Middle Easterners. A number of legal and political theorists have argued that the Anti-Terrorism Act of 1996 is specifically targeting Arab, Muslim, Middle Eastern peoples in the United States.

What are the prospects of full citizenship for Arabs-, what are the prospects for closure of the hyphen? The prospects are better now than they were before 1967, but as President Clinton's silence or reticence to act on Israel's invasion of Lebanon in April of 1996 or the October 1996 uprising in Palestine and his propensity to bomb and kill Iraqis; and as the news blackout on the presidential candidacy of Ralph Nader [an Arab American of Lebanese descent] all indicate, the hyphen is still open.

Arabs- are portrayed as submissive to Islam, to religious fanaticism, to tribalism, to patriarchs and familism, to autocrats and dictatorships, to reliving history again and again—and therefore not free: not quite free, not quite white, not quite male, not quite individual persons, not quite citizens. I argue that this is a constructed notion of the Arab- that has little to do with Arabs, with the Middle East, with Muslims, or with Arabs in America.

Events in the Middle East Fracture Arab American Unity

Yossi Shain

According to Yossi Shain, a political scientist at Tel Aviv University in Israel, Arab American identity has been forged through identification with the Palestinian cause, which has limited the impact of Arab American organizations on mainstream American politics. In this excerpt from his book, *Arab-Americans in the 1990s: What Next for the Diaspora?* Shain compares the approach taken by the integrationist Arab American Institute (AAI) (which favors getting Arab Americans elected to office regardless of their party affiliation) to the approach of the American-Arab Anti-Discrimination Committee (ADC). Shain prefers the work of the AAI—which has joined with American politicians to work toward peace in the Middle East—over that of the ADC, which he believes has been isolated from mainstream American politics by its uncompromising positions on Palestine. He also notes other issues that have threatened to weaken the political effectiveness of the Arab American community. These issues include the Gulf War of 1991, which pitted Arab countries against one another and therefore divided the loyalties of Arab Americans, and the resurgence of Muslim identity, which could potentially siphon off Muslim Arab Americans into Muslim organizations, dividing them from Christian Arab Americans.

Yossi Shain, *Arab-Americans in the 1990s: What Next for the Diaspora?* Tel Aviv: Tel Aviv University, 1996. Reproduced by permission of Tel Aviv University, The Tami Steinmetz Center for Peace Research.

In general the pattern of unequivocal diaspora [Arab American] support for the home-nation as a whole excludes the unusual circumstances when the old country and the new country are at conflict or war, a situation that brings the bewildering diaspora loyalty dilemma to its extreme. The Persian Gulf War [of 1991] resulted "in one of the worst setbacks for the Palestinians in modern times" [according to Philip Mattar]. In the United States the diaspora organizational structure was shaken and the "perils of hyphenation" [a term from an *Economist* article] reached new heights as leaders of the Arab-American community were questioned by the FBI about their knowledge of international terrorism. In reality, the diaspora was highly polarized on the question of American intervention in the Gulf [to oust Saddam Hussein's Iraqi forces from Kuwait]. A survey of Arab-Americans during the first week of February 1991 showed that the notion of Arab-American ethnic convergence on foreign policy matters was more of myth than fact. [According to researchers Sandoval and Jendrysik,] "Arab-Americans of Muslim [sic] religion were one and one-half times as likely to oppose the war than non-Moslems," and "those of Jordanian or Palestinian origin were more than twice as likely to oppose the war than other Arab-Americans.". . .

With Arab-American loyalty and patriotism called into question, Osama Siblani, the publisher of the Detroit newspaper *Sada al-Watan (The Arab-American News)* declared, "For Arab-Americans, this is their first country. America is where they chose to live. They fled persecution, oppression and poverty." Faced with the agonizing reality that Arab unity was illusory and frustrated by the Palestinian embrace of Saddam, . . . activists were torn between the pressure to affirm their American allegiance and their concern for events abroad. Moreover, "the Ambassadors of the Gulf countries in Washington made sure that of the

[Arab-American] groups they assisted in various ways, only those leaders and those organizations which supported their political position in the crisis were allowed to remain in operation" [according to M. Kay Siblani]. Thus AAI [Arab American Institute] and NAAA [National Association of Arab Americans], heavily dependent on their Gulf connections, maneuvered uneasily between supporting U.S. intervention to restore the government of Kuwait, and requiring American "consistency" towards Israel and the Palestinians. ADC [American-Arab Anti-Discrimination Committee] scored some political points among the grass-roots community by opposing the American build-up in the Gulf. Palestinian intellectuals, true to form, were "virtually silent about missed opportunities and PLO [Palestine Liberation Organization] corruption and blunders, including in the Gulf crisis."

For years, diaspora organizations had stifled serious dialogue about intra-Arab conflicts or on Arab authoritarianism: clinging to the Palestinian cause was comforting, it remained the preeminent litmus test of loyalty. After the Gulf War and the beginning of the peace process launched in Madrid [in 1991], some integrationists concluded that their domestic political empowerment could no longer remain in the sole service of Palestinian interests. In a speech delivered to a meeting of the Democratic National Committee's National Platform Committee in Cleveland, Ohio, in May 1992, James Zogby [founder of the Arab American Institute] declared that Arab-Americans should not be considered "a single-issue constituency," that they want to be heard not only on the Middle East but also on multicultural education and the broad subject of ethnic relations in the United States. . . .

Even though the voice of pan-Arabism has long been in decline in the Middle East, it has been kept alive and well among Arab-Americans. Yet, by 1995, the fragile unity between different diasporic camps, which had held together under the banner of the Palestinian cause, was dissipating rapidly, thereby threatening the vitality of Arab-American institutions and complicating further the question of Arab-American identity. In theory, the Middle East peace process should have provided Arab-Americans with a unique opportunity to end their stigmatization inside the United States and accelerate their integration into American politics. It should also have enhanced their stature as a foreign policy lobby, as they would no longer be in constant confrontation with Jewish-Americans. Yet with the passage of time we are witnessing a process of intensified diasporic fragmentation and Arab-American organizational turmoil which weakens the political vitality of the diaspora and complicates further the question of Arab-American identity. Indeed, just as it seemed to reach its apex, the Arab-American lobby found itself in a deep crisis.

This deterioration of hard-won Arab-American solidarity is closely linked to events in the Middle East and to America's foreign policy. It also reflects important transformations within the community itself: on the one hand, accelerated integration which is prevalent among American-born Christians and Muslims alike; on the other hand, among Arab Muslims, especially the younger generation, a growing shift is discernable away from Arab nationalism to Muslim identity. The revival of Islam is often encouraged by recently arrived immigrants and exiles who tend to observe the faith more strictly as a way of asserting their sense of communal identity while abroad. Indeed, Muslim groups have drawn support from younger generation Arabs disenchanted with mainstream Arab-American politics. Moreover, paradoxically, some of the immigrants who have sought refuge in the United States from the tumult of Islamic revivalism in their homeland, find themselves, because of the hardships of assimilation into American society, drawn into a devout and often militant Muslim environment.

At the time of this writing (summer 1995), mainstream diasporic activists were anxious about the shift to Islamic identification which leaves out the Christian Arabs, who still form the majority among Arab-Americans. "The next few years belong to the Islamists," said Khalil Jahshan, executive director of the near-defunct NAAA [National Association of Arab Americans]. When I visited the NAAA's office in April 1995, its staff had been cut dramatically after Arab governments slashed their funding. "Arab-Americans lack the cementing factors," Jahshan said, "We were unable to connect with our constituencies [while] Islam presents an appealing option especially to the immigrants," he added. Yet, he said, "Islam is lacking a national leadership to harness the feeling of frustration." Other integrationists, like Zogby, express greater confidence: "We are reaching more and more young people on campuses. They are proud of their Arab heritage and wish to learn more about their ancestral cultures. . . We are part of America." Osama Siblani, publisher of the *Arab American News* in Dearborn argues that in the long run, even radicalized Muslims are turning into mainstream Americans. "The ADC, the AAI and the NAAA were out of touch with the community." he said. "Their failure should enable local communities to build a more genuine Arab-American identity with an American focus." "Before making a change in Washington we must affect policy in Lansing [Michigan]." Siblani also said that "Arab-Americans, Christians and Muslims, liberals and conservatives, are becoming more powerful every day." Kay Siblani, his American wife, the executive editor of *The Arab American News*, was less certain: "The tribal and village mentality still dominates . . . Power comes from family lineage and not from what you do in America." Altogether, it is too early to determine how enduring is the current identity wave among Arab-Muslims from nationalism to religion. As always, political developments in the Middle East, including the Palestinians' ability to consolidate a secular-democratic political entity, will influence the trend abroad.

The Arab-American Left Changes Focus

Meanwhile, the Arab-American left is encountering great difficulties finding a receptive audience for their message. Far from being the rallying point it was several decades ago, it has been neutralized by the PLO-Israel accords[1] on the one hand and the Islamic challenge on the other: on many campuses across the United States, AAUG [Association of Arab-American University Graduates] is being bypassed as Arab students join Islamic groups. As late as the fall of 1993, AAUG members were still considered PLO's "ambassadors to the American people." In his message to AAUG's 26th annual convention . . . Arafat expressed confidence that his diasporic footsoldiers "will spare no effort, individually, as AAUG members, and collectively as an association, to render your service whenever duty calls. . . ." But as the initial euphoria of the peace process evaporated, and progress on the Israel-PLO track lagged, the left, consisting mainly of a shrinking group of Palestinians, and the marginalized ADC, were trying to return to their old mode; that is, blaming Israel and the U.S. for conspiring against the Arabs and the Palestinians. Like others in the Palestinian camp who had championed Arafat and the PLO for so long, the diasporic left was ready to declare "the father of Palestine" a "traitor."

Many within the AAUG feared that their organization might be compromised by Arafat's dramatic shift.

---

1. Since this article was written, peace negotiations between Israelis and Palestinians broke down in 2000. This resulted in the second Intifada, or Palestinian uprising, which has led to escalating suicide attacks on Israel and Israeli reprisals in the Palestinian territories it has reoccupied.

All in all, without the umbrella of the PLO, and in the absence of any viable leadership on the Palestinian left to fill the void, intellectuals like [Edward] Said could provide only limited rhetorical solace. In his presidential address to AAUG's annual convention in November 1994, Dr. Ziad J. Asali, asking "Where did we go wrong?" called upon his colleagues to reexamine their convictions:

> It will not do to lay blame solely on imperialism and Zionism to explain away the current state of disarray and degradation across the Arab world. It will not do to formulate slogans and generalization as a substitute for realistic strategies and thought out tactics. . . The suppression of free expression across the Arab world adds an extra measure of responsibility on the shoulders of the Arab intellectuals in the West who are not encumbered by government or violent censorship. . . For most of this century there evolved a consensus that the solution lies in pursuit of Arab nationalism and socialism. This consensus does not hold.

In fact, even Edward Said seems to have undergone an intellectual metamorphosis as he advanced a Western type condemnation of Arab and Palestinian cultures. . . . In a keynote address before the ADC's 11th National Convention Said called on Arab-Americans to capitalize on their freedom in the United States and to rescue the Arab culture from Arab leaders and governments: "[They] not only abandoned their responsibilities for the care of their people, but they have also abandoned their culture and history."

Integrationists Seek a Voice on U.S. Foreign Policy

Finally, many integrationists remain committed to the peace process and trying to assist their kinfolk in the West Bank and Gaza through economic ventures. "I look at [our venture] as Americans working for peace, helping the

economy of a region that has been war-torn," said Talat
Othman, a Palestinian-American businessman and founder
of the Chicago Arab-American Business and Professional
Association. Since the launching of the Madrid conference
in 1991, integrationist leaders have called for parity between Arab- and Jewish-Americans when it comes to Middle East affairs. They were encouraged when President
[George H.W.] Bush summoned their representatives to
the White House in November 1991 and asked them to
support his peace initiative in the region. The mainstream
was also gratified that Secretary of State Warren Christo-
pher briefed them on his trips to the Middle East, just as
he did the Jewish leadership. Certainly, soon after the
PLO-Israel accords, Arab-American integrationists seemed
to be on their way to acquiring a meaningful voice in U.S.
foreign affairs. Not long after the PLO-Israel accords were
signed, James Zogby noted that "never before has the Arab
American community had such a constructive ongoing dialogue with a Presidential administration on domestic and
foreign policy issues." Zogby . . . accompanied American
high officials like U.S. Commerce Secretary Ron Brown on
their tours of the Middle East and were invited to be
among President Bill Clinton's entourage in the signing of
the Israeli-Jordanian peace treaty. . . .

Like other ethnic diasporas in America that wish to
have an influence on U.S. foreign policy, Arab-Americans
have been "commissioned" by the American decision-
makers to export and safeguard American values and interests abroad. They are also expected to assume the role
of moral conscience of their homelands. Zogby, for example, understood that in order to sustain the reliability
of the AAI the group must show greater commitment
when it comes to democratizing Arab autocratic regimes.
The new status of mainstream Arab-American organization has also forced them to confront more assertively their

diasporic kinfolk who advocate Islamic radicalism or left-oriented rejectionism.

In anticipation of this new role the AAI held in January 1994 a conference entitled "Challenges 94: Making Democracy Work at Home and Abroad." Zogby warned that silence on issues of democracy in the Middle East would compromise Arab-Americans' political credibility, and added:

> I feel deeply that this period requires a new way of thinking—a new paradigm. If the peace accords are to bear fruit then we must make every effort to begin to develop new priorities. [While] we are [still] committed to Palestinian statehood . . .[and]oppose Israel's occupation of the Arab land . . . we [also] want to see human rights and democracy in the Arab world.

Yet any serious call for democracy in the Arab world may alienate AAI's Arab benefactors. Indeed, Zogby has already restrained his pro-democracy oratory as he now calls for an Arab-American alliance with pro-American Arab regimes: "[Arab Americans] are [Arab leaders'] strongest supports (sic) and our strength and theirs are intimately related to one another." When asked about his apparent desertion of the theme of Middle East democracy, he hailed the democratic advances that he had witnessed in his visits to Saudi Arabia. This shift is unlikely to impress the many in the Arab-American community who often call Zogby an opportunist and self-promotor.

Building Bridges After September 11

Part I: Samar Ali; Part II: Samar Ali,
interviewed by the *Washington File*

In the days following the terrorist attacks of September 11,
2001, Arab Americans, like all Americans, experienced
shock and anger, grieved for loved ones, and helped in the
rescue efforts. However, because all nineteen of the terrorists were Muslims from Arab countries, Arab American
Muslims had a special burden to bear. Some Americans
questioned their loyalty, while others took out their anger
by committing hate crimes against anyone who "looked"
Arab or Muslim. Arab American Muslims were upset that
Islam, which condemns the murder of innocent people and
whose very name includes the Arabic root for the word
peace, was used to justify the attacks. One Arab American
Muslim who publicly expressed her sentiments at the time
was Samar Ali, an American-born woman whose parents
were from Palestine and Syria, who was then a student at
Vanderbilt University in Nashville, Tennessee. Her views
are offered in the following speech and interview. On September 13, 2001, she addressed the student body of six
thousand students, expressing her pride as an American
and her condemnation of the terrorist acts as a Muslim. In
February 2002 she was elected president of Vanderbilt's
student government. In an interview for the *Washington
File*, a publication of the U.S. State Department, Ali talks
about her work on campus, including her efforts to educate
fellow students about Arabs and Muslims, to foster dialogue

Part I: Samar Ali, "Arab American Community to 'Come Together' After 9/11," *Washington File*, June 28, 2002. Part II: Samar Ali, interviewed by the *Washington File*, "Arab
American Muslim Leads Vanderbilt Student Government," *Washington File*, July 3, 2003.

among students of all faiths and backgrounds, and to urge other Arab American students to help bridge the growing divide between America and their Arab homelands.

I

I was asked to speak to you all today as an Arab-American Muslim. All I know to do is to tell you something from my heart, and my heart is filled with pride to be a student of this amazing Vanderbilt community. Look at us; we are a family. I am proud to be an American and to feel the patriotism right here, right now.

Several people have asked me how I feel as an Arab-American Muslim. When I saw my country's buildings come tumbling down with thousands of my fellow citizens on Tuesday, I felt angry as an American at whoever did this. How could somebody do this to our country and feel so much hatred towards us?

The other part of me felt upset as a Muslim. I thought, "My God, did somebody really do this in the name of my religion?"

I want everyone to know that Arabs and Muslims around the world condemn this act. I received over 40 phone calls on [Sept 11] from Arab Americans, Palestinians, and people in Syria and Jordan. They all wanted to know if America was going to be O.K. The Middle East joins the world in grieving for what has happened in America.

We cannot let these terrorists succeed and fill our hearts with hatred. We cannot allow them to split us apart as Americans. We must come together, we have come so far. We must not fight hate with hate.

The people who did this are a disgrace to mankind. While they claim to be fundamentalist Muslims, they are of no religion at all. I know of no true religion that celebrates a loss of lives. Islam condemns these acts. The people who did this do not represent any true religion or any ethnic group. These are individual attacks, and they are horrific and absolutely terrifying and must be prevented.

II

Washington File: In the election campaign, was your faith or ethnic heritage an issue to the students?

Samar Ali: I really do not think that my faith or ethnic heritage allowed me to lose or gain votes. I think my running mate Ross Lucas and I were elected for what we stood for on campus and what we could bring to the student body and help serve as the link in representing student concerns to the faculty and administration.

Anyways, during the campaign, what wasn't an issue? I mean it was a political campaign, come on. Just kidding! You are going to laugh, but you know what the biggest issue was? Whether or not I was [a member of a Sorority].

Sororities and Fraternities are a big part of social life on college campuses, and I am not in a sorority. So, my running mate and I were mostly concerned that the fact that I was not in a sorority would hurt me. We represented many different groups on campus and were able to bring in wide support. For example, even though we are both from Waverly, Tennessee, we brought diversity in that he was in the Engineering School, while I am enrolled in Arts and Sciences, he is a male and I am a female, he is in a fraternity and I am an independent (that is what we are called if we are not in a sorority or fraternity), I am Arab American and Moslem, and he is White Anglo-Saxon Protestant.

Increasing Interaction on Campus

What was your campaign's platform? Is one of your goals to increase interaction and dialogue between Muslim and non-Muslim students?

Our campaign platform was to get more students involved in Vanderbilt and to express their opinions and become more involved in the democratic process. Our theme was "Get in the Game." Also we wanted people to join us as a team and to work together as one. We kept stressing that the more people that become involved, the more we can get accomplished and the louder student needs and concerns can be heard . . .

Of course increasing interaction and dialogue between Muslims and non-Muslim students is part of the big picture as people who want everyone represented. We want more interaction between everyone. I have failed as a leader if I cannot get our Muslims on campus to open up and talk to the non-Muslims on campus and feel comfortable and vice versa, we want to provide the type of environment so that non-Muslims feel comfortable going and conversing or socializing with Muslim students. Personal contact helps break down the barriers that often cause dehumanization and hatred and a lack of understanding.

By seeing a side you only read about, the picture you see reading might change or become clearer. Interaction and dialogue through education is key. What better place to learn about other cultures and ideas than in an academic environment. The time is now. Thus, we want as many people involved and interacting as possible.

Reacting to September 11, 2001

What was going through your mind and through the minds of your Arab-American friends on September 11?

Personally, I was extremely upset. For example, of course, I felt a deep and sickening sadness for the loss of civilian lives. I just kept thinking how awful it must have been for all of those people and for their families.

Confusion was also running through my mind in respects to the idea that I could not understand how on earth people could foster so much hate that they would resort to such enormous destruction.

Vulnerability is another adjective that I would definitely use to describe both myself and several of my Arab-American friends. As an American I was concerned that there would be another attack and also about the depth of the scar it would leave on this country. In addition, as an Arab, I could not help but remember what I had learned in history class about what happened to the Japanese-Americans living in the United States after Pearl Harbor.[1] Ignorance and not learning from history can be a terrible thing, especially when combined with revenge and hate.

Thus, I was worried that many of my fellow citizens, would not realize that just because my friends and I are Muslims and Arabs, did not mean that we were part of or even agreed with the terrorists who caused September 11. We didn't even consider the terrorists to be Muslims. I was worried that people would confuse Islam with Osama Bin Ladin[2] and his agenda, that they would confuse his agenda as the agenda of all believers in Islam.

I think most Arab Americans realized that there were going to be several questions about us and who we are, and we needed to be ready to teach the truth and to help clear up the confusion that had been caused. I was afraid of the stereotypes that would be formed. Vilifying stereotypes are a catalyst for disaster. Arab Americans are relatively "new," in that most of us did not start immigrating to the United States until the 1970s.[3] Like all things, it takes time to tell your story and what you are about to your neighbors in a language that everyone can understand.

In my opinion, Al Qaeda[4] is trying to ruin Islam's rep-

1. In 1942 more than one hundred thousand Japanese immigrants and Japanese American citizens were forced into internment camps during World War II.   2. Osama Bin Ladin is a Saudi who established the terrorist organization Al Qaeda from his base in Afghanistan in the 1990s.   3. Arabs have been immigrating to America for well over a century. From 1965 to 1992 more than four hundred thousand immigrants came to America from a variety of countries.   4. Members of the terrorist network Al Qaeda planned the terrorist attacks of September 11, 2001.

utation and we are simply not going to let them win this fight. If someone has a political agenda, they need to call it what it is, and not disguise it in the name of a religion or use the religion to achieve their political goals. This is simply unacceptable.

Informing the Campus About Arabs and Muslims

You are involved with the Arab American Anti-Discrimination Committee and Middle Eastern Student Association at Vanderbilt. What kind of events/activities do they have on campus? Do you find a lot of interest or participation from the broader student body?

The Vanderbilt Middle Eastern Student Association is an organization which a Saudi Arabian student and I founded my freshman year in 1999. The Arab American Anti-Discrimination Committee has these student groups at several different colleges around the country. We had a little bit of a rocky take-off, but it is running pretty smoothly and attendance is higher than ever before. We are funded by the University. We have several members from all over the world. We have both Arab Muslims and Arab Christians. We have members who are White Anglo-Saxon Americans, Egyptians, Lebanese, Palestinians, Jordanians, Syrians, Saudi Arabians, Kuwaitis, Iranians, African Americans, and Iraqis. We also have people from Oman, Qatar, and the United Arab Emirates.

We often do co-sponsorships with the Indian-American organization on campus, the Asian-American organization on campus, the Hispanic-American organization on campus, the Malaysian group on campus, and with the Student Government Organization.

Annually we bring a speaker to campus. This year our guest speaker was [author and media critic] Dr. Jack Shaheen. He addressed media and Hollywood stereotyping of

Arabs and Moslems in America. We had over 250 people attend the lecture.

We also have an annual Middle Eastern Night where we have free Arabic food on the central lawn on Vanderbilt's campus. Vanderbilt also lets us set up a market place similar to the typical market places you see in the streets in most Arab countries, and then we have a two hour show where we put on various performances varying from an Arab band to the traditional Arab debka dance, a fashion show illustrating the different traditional wear varying from one Middle Eastern county to the next, and plays which show Arab culture.

In addition to these one-time annual events, we also hold educational sessions every month. We call them study breaks and we also have a couple of forums during the day throughout the year. The study breaks are when we go to people's dorms, provide food, and set up a round table discussion where we discuss with them for an hour about politics, religions commonly practiced in the Middle East, and Middle Eastern culture and answer any questions they might have. Many times it is a question/answer session and we also bring literature to hand out as well.

Taking the Lead After September 11

Were Vanderbilt students more interested in Islam and Muslims after September 11? If so, did you and other Muslims on campus become more proactive in explaining your faith?

For the most part, I would definitely have to say that Vanderbilt students as a majority were more interested in Islam and Muslims and Arabs after September 11. There was a class offered for the Spring Semester just on this subject, and over 200 students enrolled and people were even standing in line to be on the waiting list. This sent a message to me that people did want to learn about Islam and the followers of Islam and also about Middle East politics and history.

As for Arabs and Muslims as individuals on campus, we definitely became more mobilized and proactive. There was no other choice. As I mentioned earlier, we have a story to tell and if it goes untold, this is doing a disservice to simply everyone. We had more study breaks, more educational forums, and gave more interviews to the school newspaper than we had before. I must also at this time comment on how the attendance to these activities from the Vanderbilt student body was very high. We had at least 40 people at these question and answer sessions and also we had about 500 people (total throughout the night) come to the Middle Eastern Night.

Vanderbilt University also provided the type of atmosphere that made us feel at ease to do these kinds of activities. The administration was very amiable. Several faculty and administrators attended our events and co-sponsored our guest speaker.

Most students were concerned about how Americans were perceived and I constantly was asked how they could let Arabs know that they wanted to bridge whatever gap might exist between the two cultures. Many told me that they wanted to go with me and visit the Middle East the next time I go. My friends often asked me how my family was doing and if they were safe.

As much as I wish this was how every single student and person reacted, unfortunately that is not the case. As in almost every single society, you do have the ignorant or the people who refuse to see the big picture and carry hate inside their hearts and are content with this. As I said, while I did not encounter these kinds of comments often, occasionally they did arise. . . . I was simply shocked, but that just made me realize that there was more work that was needed to be done on all sides. Extremism never solves anything. Dehumanization is a curse. . . .

Arab Americans as Mediators

Do you have any ideas on how to improve communication between American Muslims and Arabs and the Arab/Islamic world? Do you see a special role for your community in bridging gaps of misunderstanding?

Absolutely, it is key. The world is a smaller place and therefore if countries want to succeed it seems that the more communication with other countries the better and thus the more understanding rather than misunderstanding between countries, the easier things will be. Therefore, there is a very special role for the Arab American community and the Muslim American community. We have an understanding for both cultures (Arab and Muslim and American) and can speak the languages of both. We know where both are coming from and we have also seen the human sides of both.

For example, I personally feel compassion for each side. Both sides have strong positives and it just takes people who see and deeply know that to educate others and to illustrate this and tell their story. Arab Americans have the opportunity to educate Americans about Arabs and we have the chance to tell our family and friends when we go to our native countries about American lifestyle and what kinds of lives we live and what America is like other than what might be shown by satellite.

Arab Americans have a responsibility to represent both sides to both sides. We also must stress the importance of education. Education and acceptance are key. Arab American leaders have an opportunity here to help lead both sides to a place where the world is calmer.

As I said, when you don't know someone of a particular background, it becomes easier to tear down the people, than if you see that they are people, too, just trying to live life. I have just as good a time sitting down with my friends from my hometown in Waverly, Tennessee as I do with my friends in Ramallah. Many times, we talk about the same things, and they have the same concerns and interests about school, social activities, dreams and ambitions, and movies. And in those conversations, I answer the questions in Waverly about if I only ride camels when I go over to the Middle East, and in Ramallah I answer the questions about if it is true that all Americans have lives similar to that of the characters on "Beverly Hills 90210." Also, I answer the more serious questions like whether or not both sides really truly hate the other and especially the question on both sides of, "Why do they hate us?"

Thus, I see Arab Americans taking on more of a role as mediators and people who are bridge builders. I know this might sound like utopia, and I do not think that utopia exists, but I do think that if we keep our goals high, and continue to not settle for a situation where there is more chaos than actual structure, then we will get to a point where life is better for everyone even though a few soar spots might exist. What that point is and when we will get there, well I just don't have an answer to that question.

In order to do this, I think that American Muslims and Arabs must always remember their roots and where their family is from and develop a care for both America and for their native lands. They should never turn their back on either. My parents always taught us to never forget where we came from and to never forget where we are now. It always breaks my heart when I see Arab Americans never going back and visiting the Middle East or not even acknowledging that they are Middle Eastern. I would be ashamed of myself if I felt that way. Thank God I do not. I always cherish my visits to my grandfather's house in Amman, Jordan every summer.

Most of my Arab American friends will tell you the same exact thing. About 20 of us take a trip together each summer to a different area in the Middle East. Last year we went to Syria, and this year we are going to Egypt. We always try to mix the best of both cultures (American and Arab). It is always interesting to say the least.

This reminds me of what one of my friends said to me 6 days after September 11. He said, "Samar, I think it is time you choose between being an Arab and being an American." What he simply just didn't understand is that there is no need for separation. I will always be Arab and I will always be American and I will always be Muslim.

America's War Against Terrorism and the Arab American Community

Louise Cainkar

In the weeks following the terrorist attacks of September 11, 2001, some Americans took out their anger by committing acts of violence against Arab Americans. According to Louise Cainkar, however, the most problematic response for the Arab American community was the reaction of the U.S. government, which, as a means to ensure America's safety, passed legislation that has been used to target Arab Americans. The Department of Justice and the Immigration and Naturalization Service receive heavy criticism from Cainkar, a research fellow at the University of Illinois at Chicago, for making Arab Americans and Arab visitors to America the subject of special scrutiny for no other reason than their ethnic background. Cainkar believes this prejudicial treatment rests on a long history of anti-Arab racism in America and is currently supported by a broad spectrum of Americans, especially those on the political right. Despite these troubles, Cainkar sees hope for Arab Americans. In the aftermath of September 11, Cainkar sees an increased yearning on the part of Americans to learn more about Islam and Arab culture. This trend works toward the inclusion, rather than exclusion, of Arab Americans in American life.

Unlike other ascribed and self-described "people of color" in the United States, Arabs are often hidden under the

Louise Cainkar, "No Longer Invisible: Arab and Muslim Exclusion After September 11," *Middle East Report*, vol. 224, Fall 2002, pp. 22–29. Copyright © 2002 by MERIP. All rights reserved. Reproduced by permission.

Caucasian label, if not forgotten altogether. But eleven months after September 11, 2001, the Arab-American is no longer invisible. Whether traveling, driving, working, walking through a neighborhood or sitting in their homes, Arabs in America—citizens and non-citizens—are now subject to special scrutiny in American society. The violence, discrimination, defamation and intolerance now faced by Arabs in American society has reached a level unparalleled in their over 100-year history in the US.

Rise in Anti-Arab Hate Crimes

In the seven days following September 11, Arabs and South Asians reported 645 "bias incidents and hate crimes." According to the Council on American Islamic Relations, the post-September 11 anti-Muslim backlash has been characterized by a higher degree of violence than in prior years, and includes a number of murders. In Chicago, more than 100 hate crimes against Arabs and Muslims, as well as persons mistaken for them, were reported to the Chicago Commission on Human Relations by the end of December 2001. On September 12, the largest predominantly Arab mosque in the Chicago metropolitan area was surrounded by a mob of hundreds of angry whites, some shouting "kill the Arabs," some wielding weapons. Local police and concerned citizens acted to protect Muslims in the area. Suburban police encouraged Muslims to close the schools affiliated with the mosque until their safety could be assured, and not to attend Friday prayers at the mosque. The schools were closed for one week, but prayer at the mosque continued. An Assyrian church on the north side and an Arab community organization on the southwest side were damaged by arson in the late fall. The rebuilt community center was again vandalized in March 2002. In the months immediately following September, Muslim women in Chicago repeatedly reported having their head scarves yanked off or being spit at on the street. Although the level of hate crimes and attacks against Arabs, Muslims and those perceived to be Arab or Muslim has sharply decreased since the fall [of 2002], vigilant media monitoring reveals that there is still at least one reported hate crime or attack each week nationwide. Arab and Muslim concerns about profiling, intolerance and the long-term effects of discrimination are increasing. Some blame the US government and its sweeping and unfocused actions in their communities for encouraging anti-Arab and anti-Muslim sentiments.

The US Government as Source of Anti-Arab Policies

Indeed, the greatest source of discrimination against Arabs and Muslims in the US today is the US government, mostly the Department of Justice and the Immigration and Naturalization Service (INS). According to a Council on American-Islamic Relations report released in April [2002], more than 60,000 individuals have been affected by government actions of discrimination, interrogation, raids, arrests, detentions and institutional closures. Secrecy, due process violations, arbitrariness, unlawfulness and abuse of power are among the terms used to describe the [George W.] Bush administration's post-September 11 activities by, among others, Human Rights Watch, the American Civil Liberties Union, the Reporters' Committee for Freedom of the Press and the US Foreign Intelligence Surveillance Court.

Public opinion polls continue to show widespread support for special treatment of Arabs in America. A poll conducted September 14 and 15 [2002] found respondents evenly divided over whether all Arabs in the US, including American citizens, should be required to carry special identity cards. Two late September [2002] Gallup polls found that a majority of Americans favored profiling of Arabs, including those who are American citizens, and subjecting them to special security checks before boarding planes. A December 2001 poll by the Institute for Public Affairs at the University of Illinois found that some 70 percent of Illinois residents were willing to sacrifice their civil rights to fight terrorism, and more than one quarter of respondents said Arab-Americans should surrender more rights than others. A March 5, 2002 CNN/Gallup/*USA Today* poll found that nearly 60 percent of Americans favored reducing the number of admissions to the US of immigrants from Muslim countries and an August 8, 2002 Gallup poll found that a majority of the American public said that there are "too many" immigrants from Arab countries. . . .

Islam Under Attack

Though not all Arabs in the US are Muslims (some 1.5 million are Christian), the categories are often fused in the media, quite often in a manner that openly advocates the *de facto* criminalization of both overlapping groups. Statements that collapse distinctions between Arabs, Muslims and Islamists[1] . . . call for regarding all three as innately suspicious. . . . have moved into the mainstream of conservative and even moderate opinion. . . .

Islam has come under vehement attack. Critics of the National Education Association's "September 11 Remembered" website, featuring lesson plans for teachers, say the topics covered "miss the mark." Schoolchildren should be warned that the root of the problem is in Islamic teaching, according to William Lind, terrorism expert and conservative spokesperson. Right-wing Christian activists in North Carolina have filed a lawsuit to bar the University of North Carolina from assigning an interpretive work on the Quran[2]

1. Islamism is a word that defines political, as opposed to purely religious, Islam. Some Islamists espouse the creation of Islamic states through peaceful means; the terms *Islamists* and *terrorists* are therefore not synonymous.   2. The Quran, also spelled Koran, is the holy book of Islam.

by an American scholar to entering freshmen. A recently released booklet authored by evangelists Franklin Graham and Jerry Vines, entitled *Why Islam is a Threat to America and the West*, argues that Muslims "should be encouraged to leave. They are a fifth column in this country.". . .

Exclusion Before September 11

Many Arab-Americans view the post-September 11 scrutiny, denigration and harassment of Arabs living in and seeking to enter the US as something not altogether new. . . .

Research conducted in Chicago's Arab communities in the 1980s and 1990s revealed [a broad] exclusion of Arabs from American civil society, including community-based organizations, boards of directors, foundations and local political campaigns. Participation was awarded to those few Arabs who were light-skinned, and agreed to downplay their Arabness and keep quiet about US foreign policy in the Middle East. In the mid-1990s, this local exclusion was beginning to change for the better. Still, throughout the 1990s, Arab Christians and Muslims, low-income and middle-class, immigrant and American-born, shared the view that the Arab voice is largely not welcomed in American society. In Chicago, even highly educated Arab men and women explained their preference for working in small business partly as a measure to protect themselves from the pain of interacting with Anglo-Americans. . . .

As a result of exclusion and denigration in American society, the normative pattern among Arab immigrants arriving in the last 40 years and their American-born children was to develop a range of transnational identities. Global political movements affected the particulars of this identity, so that during the era that pan-Arabism was strong in the Arab world, many in the immigrant community preferred an Arab identity. They were Arabs in America. During strong nationalist periods, national identities were highlighted, so they were Palestinians in America or Jordanians in America. Many of the American-born children of these immigrants shunned a hyphenated identity, while they waited for a society more willing to incorporate them as full members of the American mosaic. Arabs who immigrated around the turn of the twentieth century, and their children, were incorporated more smoothly into American society. It helped that they were largely Christian and were considered white. Also, at the time, US government involvement in the Arab world was limited.

Not all recent Arab immigrants and second-generation Arabs responded to the inhospitable American social context in this way. Some preferred to mask their Arab identity by changing their names from Muhammad to Mike and Farouq to Fred and by organizing their social relations around non-Arabs. . . . Some were able to blend well their American and Arab sides and comfortably viewed themselves as Arab-American. This type of self-identification was usually found among college-educated members of the second generation, but it became conflict-ridden during domestic or international crises involving Arabs. Younger Arab-Americans asked themselves: "How can I be American when that means supporting the killing of my people, justified by denigrating my ethnic identity?" The exclusion of Arabs from American civil society and government meant that the answer to this painful question was sought in transnational affiliations, rather than the affiliations sought by minorities able to participate in a democracy. . . .

A Changed Way of Life for Arab Americans After September 11

[Arab American] identities are nourished by return trips to the homeland, interactions with new immigrants and foreign students and solidarities cultivated by community institutions. Ties with the homeland are maintained in material form through periodic remittances to family members and charitable donations to support local projects. Satellite television and the Internet have greatly expanded immigrants' capacity to communicate with counterparts across the globe without traveling, but technology cannot replace the importance of face-to-face encounters to the maintenance of family ties, building communities and cross-cultural exchanges and linkages. All of these homeland ties—return travel, family visits, foreign students, family reunification, remittances and charitable donations—are likely to drop significantly due to changes in policies, the social climate and Arab-American fears after September 11.

US government initiatives since September 11 are destined to have a profoundly negative impact on an already alienated community in the US. Of the roughly 20 rule changes, executive orders and laws affecting immigrants or non-immigrant visitors, 15 predominantly target Arabs. These changes have sent a chill through all of Arab America. The number of Arabs able to study, work, attend trainings, meetings and conferences in the US will probably plummet. Profiling of Arabs at US airports, including special security checks and removal from airplanes, has dampened their desire to travel domestically or abroad. In February [2002], *Arab-American Business* magazine provided special safety tips for Arab-American travelers—in a sidebar to an article entitled "Flying While Arab."[3] Overall, these policies, most of which were never subject to a Congressional vote, target millions of innocent people on the basis of their religion, country of birth or ethnicity in response to the actions of a tiny number. The fingerprinting and registry initiative announced on August 12, 2002 for persons from select Arab and Muslim countries is only the

3. The term *racial profiling* originated with the police practice of targeting African American drivers for special scrutiny. Critics of the policy said that the only crime being committed by those pulled over by the police was "Driving While Black."

latest in a string of actions targeting Muslim and Arab communities, which began with the detention of upwards of 1,200 citizens and non-citizens, most of them of Middle Eastern descent, directly after the September 11 attacks. . . .

In November [2001], the Justice Department announced its intention to interview some 5,000 individuals who came to the US from Arab and Muslim countries since January 1, 2000 on non-immigrant visas. Later, Attorney General John Ashcroft announced a second round of interviews with an additional 3,000 persons. The subject's knowledge of terrorist activity is the topic of these interviews. The Justice Department has asked local police departments to participate in interviewing the Arab residents of their towns, placing them in the position of monitoring persons they are supposed to protect.

Immigration Policies Target Arab Americans

In January 2002, the INS launched an initiative to track down and deport 6,000 non-citizen males from (unnamed) Middle Eastern countries who had been ordered deported by an immigration judge but had never left the US. There are an estimated 314,000 so-called "absconders" in the US—the vast majority from Latin America. Although less than 2 percent are Middle Eastern, they are the government's target. By May, the Justice Department reported that 585 Middle Eastern absconders had been caught. In a meeting with members of Chicago's Arab community, government officials claimed that they were not engaging in racial profiling, since other communities would be approached next.

On May 14, [2002,] Congress enacted the Enhanced Border Security and Visa Entry Reform Act. Among the many provisions of this act, which includes calls for the integration of INS databases, the development of machine-readable visas, the requirement that all airlines submit to the US the list of passengers who have boarded a plane bound for the US and stricter monitoring of foreign students, is a restriction on non-immigrant visas for individuals from countries identified as state sponsors of terrorism. . . .

On July 14, 2002, the INS announced that it will begin enforcing section 265(a) of the Immigration and Nationality Act, which requires all aliens to register changes of address within ten days of moving. There is nothing to prevent the INS from selectively enforcing this rule. . . .

On August 12, [2002,] Ashcroft announced the implementation of a program that will require tens of thousands of approved, visa-holding foreign visitors to be fingerprinted, photographed and registered upon entry to the US. The program will be implemented in selected locations on September 11, 2002 and will target Arabs and Muslims. After a 20-day testing period, it will be implemented at all US ports of entry. Arabs and Muslims so registered can only leave from ports with the registry system in place. Carl Baron, an immigration attorney and researcher at the University of Texas, commented: "Just on the basis of where a person is coming from the government is going to subject them to these measures. You're going to see fewer Middle Easterners willing to come to the United States, and I wonder if that isn't the real agenda."

A New Interest in Islam and Arab Culture

In the midst of this environment of attacks on Arab and Muslim communities, a few good things are happening. On a local level, there appears to be a marked increase in public education about Islam, largely sponsored by local nonprofit organizations. Years of Arab activists' efforts to find receptive hosts and funders for such public education suddenly bore fruit after September 11, often sponsored by institutions that had closed their doors to Arabs in the past. Curricula are being examined for their treatment of Arabs and Islam. In a major initiative supported by the Chicago Community Trust, the Chicago public school system is studying ways to reform its curriculum to include Arabs, Islam and broader treatments of the Middle East. Earlier attempts, including by the University of Chicago's Middle East Studies Center, to make these changes had been consistently rebuffed. Arabs and Muslims are being invited to speak at public forums, to engage in dialogue and to sit "at the table." A May 2002 Arab American Institute Foundation survey found that 42 percent of Arab-American respondents publicly discuss events in the Middle East more since September 11, as opposed to 14 percent who do it less. According to Muslim American organizations, the vast majority of Arabs and Muslims report experiencing special caring, kindness and often protection from persons outside their communities in the past year, despite the overall negative climate. Islamic organizations report that conversions to Islam in the US have increased significantly since September. For perhaps the first time, Islam is being recognized as an American religion. These events reveal the apparent paradox of this historical moment: repression and inclusion be happening at the same time.

But the plethora of new restrictions on immigration, which plainly zero in on Arabs and Muslims, and the continued acceptability of stereotyping about Arabs and Islam in the media and popular culture, tell a much less encouraging story. The Arab in America is no longer invisible. Neither is some of the ugliness in America, and it's not coming from Arabs and Muslims.

CHAPTER 4

Arab Americans of Distinction

COMING TO AMERICA

Kahlil Gibran

Suheil Bushrui

The writer and painter Kahlil Gibran is best known for his book *The Prophet*, which was published in 1923 and has been beloved by generations of readers ever since. Gibran left his native Lebanon, then part of the Ottoman Empire, as a young boy in 1895 and settled with his mother and siblings in Boston. There, his talents as both writer and painter were nurtured by a variety of teachers and benefactors. According to Suheil Bushrui, author of the following selection, Gibran was well suited to bridging the cultural divide between the Arab East and America. Born an Eastern-rite Christian, Gibran brought to his English-language poetry a mystical element that found a receptive audience among the literati of Boston and New York, who were already schooled in the transcendentalism of Ralph Waldo Emerson and Henry David Thoreau. Professor Bushrui, the founder of the University of Maryland's Kahlil Gibran Research and Studies Project, believes that Gibran's poetry in Arabic also influenced generations of Arab writers, encouraging them to modernize their literary tradition.

Who knows how many . . . great individuals have had their lives touched by the works of Kahlil Gibran? A putative list would include several US presidents, among them Woodrow Wilson, who told Gibran: "You are the first Eastern storm to sweep this country, and what a number of flowers it has brought!" Did Wilson's predecessor, Teddy Roosevelt, share the unbounded enthusiasm which led his sister to host a grand banquet in Gibran's honor? And when John F. Kennedy memorably exhorted Americans: "Ask not what your country can do for you, but ask what you can do for your country," was he consciously quoting words written by Gibran and addressed to the people of Syria and Lebanon half a century earlier? Or did Gibran anticipate with uncanny accuracy a President with a gift for passionate oratory who appealed as much to the hearts as to the minds of his audience?

Bestriding Two Cultures

These rhetorical questions cannot be satisfactorily answered. Indeed, they are not meant to be answered, but to point the way to a much larger question: what is the secret behind Kahlil Gibran's astonishing success in America, a success matched by no other writer whose mother tongue was not English? The answer is that he succeeded uniquely in articulating the noblest values of this great country in terms that are powerfully direct and simple terms but enlightened by his Oriental soul.

Impressed by the great technological achievements of America, and mindful of the material well-being of the majority of its citizens, Gibran viewed his adopted home from the vantage-point of his own cultural heritage and recognized that the picture was incomplete. Consequently he sought to infuse some Eastern mysticism into Western materialism, believing that humanity was best served by a man capable of bestriding the two cultures and acknowledging the virtues of each.

His English writings, especially *The Prophet*, represent the best of both worlds, a richly harmonious blend of East and West.

Gibran, however, was not only a man from the East who brought a much needed element of spirituality to the West. He equally became a man of the West, benefiting from an environment in which freedom, democracy and equality of opportunity opened doors before him as would have been possible nowhere else in the world. His achievement thus symbolizes the achievement of America herself, a nation of immigrants which through its ingenuity and largesse has created a truly international society thriving on unity in diversity.

Arrival in America

America is in some ways entitled to claim Kahlil Gibran for one of her own sons as much as his native Lebanon. For he spent only the first twelve years of his life in Bisharri, the village where he was born in 1883, before emigrating with his family to the United States. Apart from two brief return visits to Lebanon and a two-year studentship in Paris, he lived out the last two-thirds of his life, including virtually all of his adulthood, entirely on American soil. It was in New York that he died at the age of 48.

Precocious youth though he was, he could scarcely have guessed at his destiny when he and his family set out from Bisharri on the path trod by many Lebanese before them, the journey to the "Promised Land." A rosy future might well have seemed implausible when these "five bewildered emigrants" eventually arrived and settled in Boston's Chinatown. In 1895 the area was a notorious slum and a chaotic amalgam of diverse races, cultures and religions, including the largest Syrian enclave in America after New York. A hard life awaited them, especially Gibran's mother Kamila, to whom fell the task of earning enough to sustain four children, her husband having remained in Lebanon.

The young Kahlil, however, was not deterred by these unpromising beginnings. He was here to make his mark in America; but first, America was to make a significant mark upon him. His full name in Arabic was Gibran Khalil Gibran, the middle name (in its standard transliteration) being his father's as was the convention. Not long after he had begun attending the Quincy School in Boston, his teacher of English suggested that he should drop his first name and change the correct spelling of "Khalil" to "Kahlil", making it easier for Americans to pronounce. It is by this modified form of his name that Gibran's English readers have always known him; only in his Arabic writings did he revert to the original.

At this stage of his life, Gibran's command of the English language was no more than rudimentary, and the Quincy School duly placed him in a polyglot class where everyone had to start learning English from scratch. His quick wit and verve helped him to thrive, and he was no doubt well aware that few were likely to succeed in America without a good command of English. A few years later, a decade after arriving in Boston, he wrote to his cousin N'oula, about to embark on the same transatlantic journey from Bisharri. ". . . be brave and work hard so that you can speak the language," he urged his young kinsman. "After that you will find America the best place on earth."

Early Benefactors Pave the Way

By then Gibran had good reason to be grateful to his adopted country, having benefited substantially from the percipience and generosity of several Americans. First among these were Florence Pierce and Jessie Fremont Beale of Denison House, the social center or "settlement house" in Boston where Gibran's talents as an artist began to burgeon. So impressed were they by the work of the young immigrant that Jessie Beetle felt compelled to bring him to the attention of Fred Holland Day, an avant-garde photographer and publisher with an interest in nurturing gifted young people. Besides becoming Day's favorite photographic model, the adolescent Gibran gained much from the older man's guidance and support. Through him he met the poetess Josephine Peabody, another who helped his career and the first person known to have dubbed him "prophet."

By 1904 Gibran had developed sufficiently as a painter to begin exhibiting his work in Boston, with moderate success. More important than the critical reception accorded his paintings, however, was the presence of a young headmistress at one of these exhibitions; Gibran thus met the woman who became his selfless patroness, benefactress and collaborator, Mary Haskell. This prim, sensitive, dynamic schoolteacher, arguably by far the most important individual in his life over the next two decades, perhaps best personifies the bounty of America as experienced by Gibran. Yet it was an ambivalent relationship, Gibran's joyous gratitude at times turning to a burdensome feeling of indebtedness.

Such ambivalence equally characterized his attitude towards America, perhaps not surprisingly in one who longed for the place of his birth and would himself come to symbolize the struggle to reconcile East and West. The "best place on earth" in 1905 had three years later become "this mechanical and commercial country whose skies are replete with clamour and noise." A further three years on, Gibran was describing America as "far greater than what superficial people think; her Destiny is strong and healthy and eager." By June 1912 he had amplified this into the observation that

What is real and fine in America is hidden to the foreigner . . . the real splendor of America is in her ideal of health, her power to organize, her institutions, her management, her efficiency, her ambition. . . .

The Move to New York City

The years 1911 and 1912 were of great consequence for Kahlil Gibran. After two years in Paris studying art at Mary Haskell's expense, he was ready to start making a proper living from his paintings and drawings. His writings, not yet in English, were also beginning to win him some renown, albeit purely among Arab readers. It was time for him to move to New York, where the ambiance and consciousness would be better suited to his aspirations than stately Boston. Not that Boston had played an insignificant part in his intellectual and artistic upbringing. It was there that he was exposed to the transcendentalism of [Ralph Waldo] Emerson, [Henry] Thoreau and [Walt] Whitman, fashionable in 1890s Boston, and the influence of which is discernible in those of his writings which display a joyous feeling of oneness with nature. There, too, Gibran had inevitably been cast in the role of an exotic attraction, "a talented and precocious visionary who could draw like an angel." But that airy world was far behind him now, and the youth was a man of very nearly thirty years with no patience for transience or superficiality.

Gibran came to live in New York at the instigation of his fellow Lebanese émigré writer Ameen Rihani, another whose life was devoted to the promotion of East-West understanding; in 1911 he provided the illustrations for Rihani's pioneering work *The Book of Khalid*, the first attempt by an Arab at a novel in English. . . .

Although in every other sense his home would always be the much longed-for Bisharri, New York became Gibran's professional home. Crucially, New York provided him with the "fine, large studio" at 51 West Tenth Street where he was to produce his finest work, and which he dubbed "The Hermitage." He moved in early in 1913. Gibran the artist was about to recede into the shadow of Gibran the writer. One of his closest friends, his fellow Lebanese poet and philosopher Mikhail Naimy, sums up this period of the poet's life as follows:

. . . *Gibran, urged by the incessant calls for enfoldment of the twin sisters lovingly nursed by his soul—Poetry and Art—was far from being content with the small and slow conquests he was making in the world. To the American public he offered his art without his poetry. To the Arab public, his poetry without his art. The English-speaking world could not read his Arabic poetry; the Arab-speaking world could not understand his western art. The twins must be made to work as one team. For that he must write in English.*

Mastering the English Language

In his attempts to master the English language, Gibran was fortunate indeed to have the unstinting help and encouragement of Mary Haskell. As early as 1912 he told her of his determination to write in English, and his plans for two works in particular. One of these he was already calling *The Madman*, under which title it was published six years later. The other, as yet untitled and simply referred to as "My Book," was to be built around the teachings of an "Island God" in exile. This took a full eleven years to evolve into the work we now know as *The Prophet*.

Mary was used from the start as a consultant on Gibran's English writings, a role she undertook with relish. At first she was like his teacher, helping him appreciate the nuances and subtleties of idiomatic English. Gibran was no beginner, but he was a quick learner; and before long her help was confined to correcting his punctuation and grammar, and occasionally suggesting an alternative word for greater felicity of sound. Beginning in June 1914, he sought her comments on most of his English output as it was being written and rewritten: first *The Madman*, then *The Forerunner*, and finally *The Prophet*, whose publication in 1923 marked the end of their collaboration. . . .

The following lines already show traces of the style that would later become familiar to millions, as well as illustrating Gibran's attachment to the idea of the poet as prophet:

Poet, who has heard thee but the spirits that follow thy solitary path?

Prophet, who has known thee but those who are driven by the Great Tempest to the lonely grove?

And yet thou are not alone, for thine is the Giant-World of super-realities, where souls of unborn worlds dance in rhythmic ecstasies; and the silence that envelops thy name is the very voice of the Great Unknown. . . .

The Writer Meets a Publisher

In June 1918, Gibran met another of that small band of Americans who could justifiably claim to have contributed materially to his success. After *The Madman* had been refused by a number of publishers, he turned to the young and inexperienced Alfred Knopf, whose name has since become inextricably linked with that of Gibran in the minds of the reading public. "Everybody speaks highly of Knopf as a man, and also as a publisher," wrote the poet shortly before their first meeting. "He is young and has an eye for the beautiful. . . [and] he is honest—he does not leave anything unsaid," Gibran noted with approval when the contract to publish *The Madman* was signed a few days later. It was a bold gamble on Knopf's part, but his remarkable faith in a writer unknown to English-speaking readers was to be richly and deservedly rewarded. He subsequently published all of Gibran's English works including *The Prophet*, as well as several works originally written in Arabic and translated by others into English.

Both *The Madman* and *The Forerunner* enjoyed largely favorable critical reviews which ensured enough sales for Knopf to persevere with Gibran. Ironically, *The Prophet* was much less sympathetically received, gaining its vast readership almost exclusively by word-of-mouth recommendation. It was *The Madman* which established his credentials as a writer to be taken seriously in America and this was reflected in the many invitations he began receiving to read, speak or just appear at a variety of functions. . . .

In 1919 Gibran's success as an artist, which contributed in no small part to well-founded comparisons between him and the great [English] poet-painter William Blake, reached its zenith with the publication by Alfred Knopf of a volume entitled *Twenty Drawings*. The enthusiastic introduction by Alice Raphael, a leading art critic of the day, offers some illumination of this aspect of Gibran's creative genius: . . .

. . . *He senses the meaning of the earth and her productions; of man, the final and the consummate flower, and throughout his work he expresses the interrelating unity of man with nature.*

Influencing the Course of Arabic Writing

This most productive period in Gibran's life also saw him reach a peak as a writer in Arabic, with the publication in 1920 of *al-'Awasif* (*The Tempests*), a collection of short narratives and prose poems which had appeared in various journals. At the same time Gibran also became founder-president of a literary society called *al-Rabita 'l-Qalamiyya* (The Pen Bond). The original members of *Arrabitah*, as it was known for short, were all leading Arab-American writers: Mikhail Naimy, Naseeb 'Arida, Nudra Haddad, Rashid Ayyub, Ilya Abu Madi, and Gibran himself. The society was to exert enormous and lasting influence on the renaissance in Arab letters, both in America and in other parts of the globe including the Arab world itself. In particular its members developed a unified approach to Arabic literature and art, and introduced a much-needed spirit of avant-garde experiment into a largely fossilized institution. Fired by Romantic ideals of individual inspiration, pantheism and universal love, they revitalized a great literary language by bringing it closer to the colloquial. And like so many pioneers in different fields throughout history, their unfettered approach was fiercely reviled by reactionaries while being vigorously embraced by those who were hungry for innovation.

The success of what can only be described as a literary revolution, spearheaded by Gibran, was due in no small part to its genesis in New York, far away from the seat of the traditions to which it offered an unprecedented challenge. There was no Ottoman regime to oppress these writers of al-Mahjar, as the Arab literati in America were known collectively. By the same token, their very remoteness from their roots induced powerful emotions which, coupled with the many-sided influence of Western culture, inspired some exceptional poetry and prose, not least from Kahlil Gibran himself.

Few would contest Gibran's status as the greatest of Arab Romantics and father of a 20th-century Romantic tradition whose impact on Arab writers has been at least as strong as that of 19th-century figures such as Wordsworth and Keats on their English-speaking counterparts. He was not just a Romantic, however. His success as a writer in both Arabic and English gave him a platform for the expression of views which he felt his fellow Arabs needed to hear, and on occasion he could be quite didactic. His Arabic articles in the early 1920s were dominated by the message that the developing nations should "adopt only the constructive aspects of Western society." He feared that the East was either being seduced by the more dangerous attractions of the West or else turning its back altogether. . . .

A Literary Voice That Endures

The overall effect of [his literary] acceptance on Gibran was to make him feel more truly a "citizen of the world," a genuine cosmopolite bestriding both East and West. As if to underline this, in 1925 he was invited to become an officer of the New Orient Society in New York, which was dedicated to the promotion of East-West understanding. It was a singular honor, for the Society's quarterly journal, to which he was also asked to contribute, boasted a distinguished list of writers including Annie Besant, John Dewey, Bertrand Russell, H.G. Wells, and Claude Bragdon. . . .

Gibran was to complete four more books in English: *Sand and Foam, The Earth Gods, The Wanderer*, and the best of his late works, *Jesus, the Son of Man*. But the work on which his fame rests will probably always be *The Prophet*, which Mary Haskell called "the most loving book ever written.". . . Gibran not only saw himself as the teacher bringing a breath of spirituality to the West, but as the recipient of many bounties in his adopted land. . . .

The Prophet is a work of . . . universal appeal. . . . Gibran's purpose was a lofty one, and his belief in the "unity of being", which led him to call for universal fellowship and the unification of the human race, is a message which retains its potency today as do the messages of all great poets. Inspired by his experiences in a country far from the land of his origins, he strove to resolve cultural and human conflict, in the process developing a unique genre of writing, and transcending the barriers of East and West as few have done before or since. He became not only Gibran of Lebanon, but Gibran of America, indeed Gibran the voice of global consciousness: a voice which increasingly demands to be heard in the continuing Age of Anxiety.

Naomi Shihab Nye

Naomi Shihab Nye

Writer and poet Naomi Shihab Nye is an award-winning author of more than twenty volumes. Nye, who was born in 1952 to a Palestinian father and an American mother, grew up in St. Louis and San Antonio and spent a year of high school in Jerusalem. The following essay was written to introduce her anthology, *The Space Between Our Footsteps: Poems and Paintings from the Middle East*, a collection of the work of modern poets and painters. In the essay Nye extols the Arab literary heritage that nurtured her, including her father's storytelling and the lasting legacy of Arab American poet Kahlil Gibran.

If you say you are going to the Middle East, people around you often raise their eyebrows. It is quite possible that the Middle East is one of the most negatively stereotyped places on earth. How did this happen to a place which has been the center of so much dramatic cultural and religious history? Unless American adults and teenagers have lived or traveled in the region themselves, many know only what they hear in the news or see in flamboyant movies (Arabs riding out of the desert on horseback). Of course, the violent or unhappy news stories are usually the ones that get transmitted. But what a terrible fragment they are of the fuller story, which is as rich and interesting as life anywhere else.

Naomi Shihab Nye, *The Space Between Our Footsteps: Poems and Paintings from the Middle East*. New York: Simon & Schuster Books for Young Readers, 1998. Copyright © 1998 by Naomi Shihab Nye. Reproduced by permission of Simon & Schuster Books for Young Readers, an imprint of Simon & Schuster Children's Publishing Division.

We should remember that the same distortion of news is happening in the other direction, too. What do Middle Easterners hear and imagine about the United States? We are a country of murderers and drug addicts. People are afraid to walk in the streets. Families are fractured. Students are "dropping out" in all directions. We don't care about our elders, putting them in "homes" away from us. Most of us would resent such a negative portrait and would work hard to balance it.

I can't stop believing human beings *everywhere* hunger for deeper-than-headline news about one another. Poetry and art are some of the best ways this heartfelt "news" may be exchanged.

An Arabic Heritage

As an Arab-American child growing up in the United States, I never read anything remotely connected to my father's first culture, except perhaps [the folktales collected in] *The Arabian Nights*. This book hardly felt much like our *lives*.

Luckily, I had a fair imagination and our Palestinian father was a wonderful storyteller. Every night my brother and I drifted off to sleep wrapped in the mystery of distant neighbors, villages, ancient stone streets, donkeys, and olive trees. Our house by day was fragrant with cardamom spice and coffee, pine nuts sizzled in olive oil and delicious cabbage rolls. My girlfriends brought iced cupcakes to Girl Scouts for treats, but I brought dates, apricots, and almonds. Arabic music on scratchy records filled the air in our home.

I wasn't yet sure where the sense of "other" began in the human heart or how many variations and shadings the larger family could contain. But I didn't fear differences. In fact, I loved them. This is one of the best things about growing up in a mixed family or community. You never think only one way of doing or seeing anything is right.

The Literary Legacy of Gibran

After beginning high school in Jerusalem, which altered my perception of the universe irrevocably, then returning to the States to live in Texas, I began reading books by Khalil Gibran, one of the best-selling authors of all time. Teenagers often identify with his ruminative tone, lyrical philosophies, and eloquent sense of contradiction. I used to smuggle *The Prophet* into my homemaking class wrapped in the denim dress I was sewing. I would read it between stitches.

"Only when you drink from the river of silence shall you indeed sing" and "Your children are not your children. /They come through you but not from you, /And though they are with you, yet they belong not to you . . . /You are the bows from which your children as living arrows are sent forth. . ." [wrote Gibran].

Gibran came to the United States from Lebanon when he was 27 and devoted himself to writing in both Arabic and English, and to painting and drawing. Though he died at a relatively young age (48), his work outlives him in a powerful way, continuing to appear in new editions. The only park dedicated to a writer in Washington, D.C., was dedicated, within the past decade, to Gibran. It sits across the road from the Vice President's house. I think Gibran would be very happy to know that other Arab-American writers have been finding one another the past 20 years and a slowly, but steadily increasing, body of work by Middle Eastern writers is being made available to readers in the United States.[1] We toast Gibran for his devotion and example.

The history of literature and art in the Middle East extends back countless generations. In tribal times poetry

1. For some recent anthologies of Arab American writing see Gregory Orfalea and Sharif Elmusa, eds., *Grape Leaves: A Century of Arab-American Poetry.* New York: Interlink Books, 2000; and Munir Akash and Khaled Mattawa, eds. *Post-Gibran Anthology of New Arab American Writing.* Syracuse, NY: Syracuse University Press, 1999.

was recited around a blazing fire—a popular early tradition was the spoken add-on poem in which each voice contributed new lines, in turn. Repetition, passionate rhythm, and melodrama were admired. . . .

Consider *The Space Between Our Footsteps* to be like the *mezza* tables of hors d'oeuvres spread out all across the Middle East, which often precede a greater feast—tiny, delicious plates of *hummos* and *baba ghanouj*, elegantly decorated with sprigs of mint and dashes of paprika, *tabbooleh*[2] salad, pickled turnips, cucumbers and tomatoes, heaps of bread . . . guests dip in from all directions.

With writers and artists from Algeria, Bahrain, Egypt, Iran, Iraq, Israel, Jordan, Kuwait, Lebanon, Libya, Morocco, Oman, Palestine, Qatar, Saudi Arabia, Syria, Tunisia, Turkey, United Arab Emirates, and Yemen, our book has tried to represent the wide, delicious feast. . . .

While some who like to classify might describe Middle Eastern poetry as being heavily embellished or romanticized and Middle Eastern art as being primarily abstract, this book hopes to extend that notion. Subjects include an immense affection for childhood and children, a tender closeness to family, a longing for early, more innocent days, a passion for one's homeland, grief over conditions of exile (a situation too common through the centuries to many Middle Easterners), a reverent regard for the natural world, and a love for one another and for daily life. Do any of these concerns sound alien to us?

Literature Takes Us Back to Our Roots

Once my husband Michael and I were sleeping soundly in our room in an old downtown hotel in Aleppo, Syria, when

---

2. *Hummos, baba ghanouj*, and *tabbooleh* are all Middle Eastern specialties that have become increasingly popular in America. *Hummos* is a dip made of chickpeas and sesame paste, called tahini. *Baba ghanouj* has the same ingredients with the addition of eggplant. *Tabbooleh* is a salad composed of bulgar wheat and a variety of vegetables, flavored with mint.

the water in our bathroom sink turned on by itself. I woke gradually to the gush of a waterfall, the encroaching roar of a fountain, and couldn't imagine where the sound was coming from.

Slowly my eyes adjusted to the stream of water pouring from the edge of the sink onto our bathroom floor. It rolled riverlike into the bedroom so the rugs beside our bed were already soaked. I leapt into the bathroom and attempted to turn off the water. The faucet spun uselessly in my hand. How had this happened? Did our room have ghosts?

I grabbed the telephone. But my *SOS* Arabic at one A.M. wasn't very good. Soon the groggy desk clerk appeared at our door with a pitcher full of drinking water, thinking I'd *asked* for some. When he saw the sea growing rapidly around us, he awakened quickly, racing back to the old-fashioned metal-cage elevator with its ornate grillwork. He returned soon with a mop, a bucket, and a basket of rags and the three of us set to work, joined in our cause, until Michael pointed out it might be a good idea to turn off the water valve under the sink. We'd all been too sleepy to think of it.

The valve was stuck. The clerk ran for pliers. What happened next was like a dance, three people mopping, dipping, laughing, wringing out the rags, soaking our pajama cuffs and socks. The clerk shrugged when I kept asking him in my bumbling Arabic how this could have happened. Weren't we in the Middle East? Wasn't water something of a premium in these ancient lands? Maybe this was one of the springs that used to rise up suddenly between stones in my father's folktales.

We fell asleep again. At 4:30 A.M. our telephone rang and the clerk, now our good buddy, said someone was downstairs waiting for us. A plumber? We hadn't been expecting anyone. We dressed hurriedly and rode the clanky elevator down. A tall red-haired man shook our hands and introduced himself as Adlai Qudsi, architect and preservationist, who had come to give us a sunrise tour of his beloved city. We did not tell him we had already been up half the night, nor did we have the slightest inclination not to follow him.

He took us first to the famous citadel which towers over Aleppo like a castle with its fortress-wall. We could look down over the twinkling city from there. He took us walking in careful single file along the edges of rooftops to a sitting spot where we could watch the sky ease gently into its early, perfect pink. Who was this person who would dream up such an outing for people he didn't even know? He shrugged. "I heard some visitors were in town. I thought you might like to see something special." He showed us exactly where to gaze to get the best views of sky and buildings and land.

After sunrise, he knocked on doors in the Old City. Sleepy women wearing flowery aprons let us in. They obviously knew and respected Mr. Qudsi. He wanted to show us how the soft early light fell through their high arched windows, illuminating blue and green mosaic tiles. He wanted us to see a three-hundred-year-old fountain in a courtyard. Light fell onto its tower like a glittering top-hat. When we sat with Mr. Qudsi in a café for breakfast tea, we told about our water escapade and he grinned. "I'd much rather have old pipes than new buildings!" he said proudly.

This is what I want a book of poems and paintings to be—a surprising spring waking us from our daily sleep. A feast of little dishes. An unexpected walk along the rim of a majestic city. *Ahlan Wa Sahlan*—You are all welcome!

Edward Said

Edward Said

Professor Edward Said of Columbia University, who died in 2003, was a literary critic, music critic, and political activist for the Palestinian cause. Said was born in Jerusalem in 1935 and grew up in Palestine and in Egypt, where his father was a prominent businessman. After the Arab-Israeli war of 1948, members of his extended family became refugees and fled Palestine for Egypt and the United States. Said came to America in 1951 to attend boarding school and remained to study at Princeton and Harvard universities. In the following interview, recorded in 1999, Said says that it was the knowledge of his impending death from leukemia that led him to write *Out of Place*, a memoir about never quite belonging in the places where he grew up. In his work as a literary critic, Said was drawn to other exiles and outsiders, such as Polish-born novelist Joseph Conrad, who wrote novels in English about the dark side of British imperialism. Said also discusses his most famous book, *Orientalism*, in which he takes to task Western historians of the Middle East by exposing their biases and prejudices, which he believed were deeply rooted in the colonial exploitation of the region. Said comments that, inevitably, there will be many interpretations of *Orientalism*, which is now read by intellectuals worldwide.

Having completed your memoir, Out of Place, *in which you write about the need to leave behind a "subjective account" of your youth in Egypt, Palestine, Lebanon, and*

Edward Said and Moustafa Bayoumi, "An Interview with Edward W. Said (1999)," *The Edward Said Reader*, edited by Moustafa Bayoumi and Andrew Rubin. New York: Vintage Books, 2000. Copyright © 2000 by Edward W. Said. Copyright © 2000 by Moustafa Bayoumi and Andrew Rubin. Reproduced by permission of Vintage Books, a division of Random House, Inc.

the United States, you chose to focus on a period of your life before the 1967 [Arab-Israeli] war. What is the intention behind your beginning?

Edward Said: It is difficult to describe what you feel when you get a peculiar diagnosis, such as the one I received in September of 1991. I was told that I had a very obscure disease, though it is quite common among the leukemias. While I showed no symptoms, I was told that I had a sword of Damocles hanging over my head. It suddenly dawned on me that I was going to die.

I don't think that I was ever consciously afraid of dying, though I soon grew aware of the shortage of time. My first impulse was to go some place quieter than New York, but that idea didn't last very long. And then, from out of the blue, I think probably left over from the death of my mother, who died in July of 1990, I considered writing about my early years, most of them connected with her. Two and a half years later, in March 1994, I began the memoir. . . .

During the treatment, writing the memoir became a kind of discipline for me. I would use the time in the mornings to write and to follow my memory to reconstruct a world that I had lost and was losing more and more of everyday. As a way of shaping the book, I tried to recall the places that had changed irrecoverably in my life: Egypt, Palestine, and Lebanon. During that period I visited those places. I went back to Palestine in 1992 for the first time in forty-five years, and I went back to Lebanon in 1992, my first visit there since the Israeli invasion of 1982.

The Personal Versus the Political Memoir

What does it mean for you to recover loss in your own mind as opposed to responding to the objective and political experience of national loss?

With *Out of Place*, I was trying to free myself from the

responsibility that, whether I liked it or not, was imposed on me whenever I wrote about the Middle East. There was always a political issue to respond to. My whole engagement after the 1967 [Arab-Israeli] war was predicated on that basis, and I never really had time to do much else.

Out of Place was written in a setting of a certain amount of suffering. A lot of the time I was quite ill. I would write a few sentences and then I would have to get up and take some medicine, or lie down. Writing *Out of Place* was a completely different kind of experience for me. I wasn't trying to address an audience, though I had some idea of addressing my children's generation. Neither of my children knew my father, for example, whereas both of them knew my mother. The memoir was an attempt to describe my past for them and to record events and experiences that had made a great impression on me. . . .

How would you compare this to your other longer autobiographical meditation, After the Last Sky?

After the Last Sky was written in response to a particular political situation. It arose from a conference at the United Nations in Geneva in 1983 and from the fact that the United Nations would not allow us to place captions beneath the photographs of Palestinians. . . . *After the Last Sky* was a political occasion geared at reconstructing the experience and lives of Palestinians. In contrast, *Out of Place* had to do with my own sense of my life ebbing away.

Authors Who Made an Impact

You begin Out of Place *with the idea of the invention of families and of the self, which has echoes of your first book,* Joseph Conrad and the Fiction of Autobiography. *More than Foucault or Frantz Fanon, why has Conrad occupied such a central place in your writing?*

I first read, [the author Joseph] Conrad when I was about seventeen or eighteen years old as an undergraduate at Princeton. It was my freshman year, and I was reading *Heart of Darkness*, which completely mystified me at the time. It presented a kind of writing that I had never encountered before. As a child I had read a lot—Walter Scott, Conan Doyle, Alexandre Dumas, Dickens, Thackeray—and I had acquired a very strong background in what I would call not just novels of adventure, but *novels of openness*—novels where everything seems available to you. *Heart of Darkness* had the form of an adventure story, but the more I looked at it, the more the adventure story dissolved. I remember having discussions with my friends in the dormitory trying to figure out what "the horror" meant, who Kurtz was, and so forth. Sometime later, a year before I went to graduate school, I then began to read an enormous amount of Conrad, and the more I read, the more I wanted to know about him. As a graduate student at Harvard, I looked through a volume of letters that he wrote to Cunningham Graham and I was struck that there was a certain back and forth between his letters and his fiction—many of the things that appeared in his letters would turn up in a different way in his fiction.

Conrad always seems to come back to me in one way or another. I think that his exile, the overtones of his writing, its accents, its slippages, his sense of being in and out of language, being in and out of worlds, his skepticism, his radical uncertainty, the sense that you always feel that something terribly important is going on . . . a tremendous crisis happening but you can't tell what it is—has just gripped me more than any other writer has.

How did the relatively little-read Giambattista Vico come to have such marked presence in your work?

Vico was an accidental discovery through a dear friend, Arthur Gold, who was a classmate of mine at Princeton and Harvard. What interested me most about Vico was that he was self-made and self-taught. Vico represented somebody who succeeded on his own by the act and strength of his imagination. Throughout his writings, for example, there are wild and fantastic images—of giants, of men and women copulating, of ferocious settings with thunder striking, and so on. For him, imagery was inextricably related to the writing of history, and added to that was the connection between imagery and words, and how words are, at the first stage onomatopoeic—primitive imitations of emotions of fear and of disorganization. Vico completely disrupted the Cartesian paradigm [of reason].

What also attracted me to Vico was his interest in philology, and, I must say, his relative obscurity. He was a philologist, a professor of eloquence and Latin jurisprudence at the University of Naples in the early eighteenth century. The more I read about him, the more he attracted me. He led me to [literary critic] Erich Auerbach, since Auerbach had translated Vico into German. In addition, there was something private about Vico, just as there was something private about Conrad that neither one of them every fully disclosed. I focused on that and tried to make of it what I could, as a way of validating what I was trying to do outside the given academic track. Lastly, as with Conrad, I found the organization of Vico's work, *The New Science*, completely original, almost artistic. Vico was a great theoretician of beginnings.

The Emergence of Arab American Identity

Is that how you came to write Beginnings?

Beginnings is really the product of the 1967 war. I was at Columbia in the summer of 1967, and I had been awarded a fellowship at the University of Illinois, where I spent 1967 and 1968 at the Center for Advanced Study.

Around that time I was serving on a jury. The day the war began, June 5, was my first day as a juror. I listened to the reports of the war on a little transistor radio. "How were 'we' doing?" the jurors would ask. I found I wasn't able to say anything—I felt embarrassed. I was the only Arab there, and everybody was very powerfully identified with the Israelis. Also, during that summer, which I spent in New York, I became connected with the Arab political world because of the UN meetings. I started to meet diplomats, and I suddenly found myself, after sixteen years of being in this country, back in touch directly with the Middle East and the Arab world.

My project for Illinois was to be a book on [the eighteenth-century Irish author Jonathan] Swift. But when I arrived in Illinois, I found myself in a difficult situation because of the war, I became increasingly concerned about my family still in the Middle East, and became increasingly aware of a part of the world that now had been thrust upon me. Furthermore, my marriage was coming apart. One day I found myself talking about beginnings. I began writing an essay entitled "Meditation on Beginnings," which was really an attempt to reformulate where I was. . . . The question of beginnings obsessed me. I divorced the following year and began to work on a study of the relationship between beginnings and narrative, which brought me back to Vico. *Beginnings* was thus really a project of reaction to a crisis that caused me to rethink what I was doing, and try to make more connections in my life between things that had been either suppressed, or denied, or hidden.

Orientalism . . . has been a tremendously influential book, translated into many languages, but, as you write in the afterword, it has . . . become more than one book. It has been interpreted in many different ways. Why do you think this book has produced so many different reactions and readings?

Every context produces different readers and different kinds of misinterpretations. In *Orientalism*, I begin with a notion that interpretation is misinterpretation, that there is no such thing as the correct interpretation. For instance, I recently got a letter from the publisher of the Bulgarian edition of *Orientalism*, asking if I would write a preface for it. I didn't know what to say. *Orientalism* is about to appear in Hungary, in Vietnam, and in Estonia. These are all places that I've never been to and I know very little about. So you can see how uncontrolled all these interpretations can be. In that respect, I think certain kinds of distortions and deviations are inevitable.

What you *can* control is your own ideas. . . . I've been very conscious about not doing that. I've alway tried to develop my ideas further, in ways that paradoxically make them in a certain sense ungraspable and unparaphrasable. . . .

Music and the Work of the Literary Critic

Figures of silence and sound have been very important in your literary criticism. How do you think your training as a musician has affected your reading of literature?

That's a very interesting question. . . . The idea of bringing literature to performance, is certainly connected to the notion of music. The idea is that works of art place a premium on expression, articulation, clarity. All the things that we associate with writing and with performance involve a discourse that needs to be unfolded and then presented.

But at the same time, I've always been interested in what gets left out. . . . I'm interested in the tension between what is represented and what isn't represented, between the articulate and the silent. For me, it has a very particular background in the questioning of [any] document. What does the document include? What doesn't it include? . . .

In the particular case of the Palestinians, one of our problems is that we don't have documents to substantiate what we said happened to us. Take one of the Israeli new historians, Benny Morris, for instance. He's very literal-minded, and he's done very important work, but his assumption is that he can't say anything about what happened in 1947–1948[1] unless there's a document to show for it. I say, well, why not try to animate that silence? . . . Why not look at oral history? Why not look at geographical evidence? Why not look at the landscape? Why not go through the process of trying to reconstruct out of the silence what was either destroyed or excluded?

1. In 1947 the United Nations voted to divide Palestine into two states, one for the Israelis and another for the Palestinians. The Arabs opposed this plan. During the ensuing war five Arab nations attacked Israel but were defeated. By the end of the war Israel had expanded her borders to include approximately one-third to one-half of the land originally set aside for a Palestinian state. As a consequence of the war approximately 750,000 Palestinians became refugees.

Tony Shalhoub

Antoine Faisal and Lynne Vittorio

In 2003 the Arab American actor Tony Shalhoub won both an Emmy Award and a Golden Globe for his portrayal of Adrian Monk, the quirky, obsessive-compulsive detective in the television series *Monk*. After a long career on both stage and screen, Shalhoub is considered to be one of the most talented character actors at work today. Shalhoub's father emigrated from Lebanon at the age of ten, and his mother is a second-generation Lebanese American. Tony Shalhoub first appeared on stage at the age of six, when a sister arranged for him to play the part of a child in a high school production. Later, he attended the acclaimed Yale Drama School and joined the American Repertory Theater in Cambridge, Massachusetts. In this interview with Antoine Faisal and Lynne Vittorio for the Web site Aramica.com, Shalhoub says that he has avoided being typecast as an Arab by portraying a variety of ethnic characters, including Italian, Hispanic, Greek, and Jewish, but he has never been afraid to own his Arab American identity. His hopes are that in the future, films will portray the many roles Arab Americans have played in American life.

Having a regular role on a hit television series could be, for many actors, both a blessing and a curse. While providing a steady income and a tremendous amount of exposure, one also runs the risk of being pigeonholed into a certain type of role or being forever emblazoned upon the minds of viewers as one particular character. It is not unusual for many actors, after a series has ended, to never regain the exposure and the popularity they had during the time their show was on the air.

Some actors try to protect themselves from this seeming inevitability by taking on film roles during the time that their series is "hot". Often, these films bomb at the box office. Sadly, very few actors who became "stars" on a television series have been able to either cross over to film stardom or simply avoid the curse of being forever known as the character they played. Perhaps the ability to avoid that fate is one mark of a truly talented performer. It is certainly true of Tony Shalhoub.

Most of America came to know Tony through *Wings* (1991–1997), where he delighted us each week with his portrayal of the terribly sweet, more than slightly neurotic immigrant cab driver, Antonio Scarpacci. During the entire run of *Wings*, however, Tony appeared in a number of successful films (*Honeymoon in Vegas, Addams Family Values, Searching for Bobby Fischer, I.Q., Gypsy, Big Night, Men in Black, Gattaca,* and *A Life Less Ordinary*), showcasing his ability to create highly divergent characters and proving that he possessed great talent and range.

The end of *Wings* did not mark the end of Tony's career. He has continued appearing in a number of films, both comedic and dramatic, ranging from controversial (*The Siege*—which became, sadly, rather prescient) to scary (*Thirteen Ghosts*) to funny (*Galaxy Quest, Men in Black II*). He stars in and executive produces the extremely successful and enjoyable *Monk* (on USA Network), for which he won the Emmy [for best actor in a comedy series] in 2003 and for which he . . . won the Golden Globe [for best performance by an actor in a TV series].

What Tony is most excited about and proud of [in 2003] is *Made Up*, an independent film starring his wife, Brooke Adams, written and starring his sister in law, Lynne Adams, and directed by himself. It is, as its tagline says,

"A Coming of Middle Age Comedy" that has something insightful and humorous to say about mothers and daughters, sisters, romance, beauty, aging, and the surprises life has in store for all of us, regardless of age.

Born into a large Lebanese family and raised in Green Bay, Wisconsin, Tony studied theater at the Yale School of Drama and starred in numerous theatrical productions in New York before making his television debut in 1986. Tony graciously responded to our request for an interview, fitting us into his hectic schedule with little fuss. While his daughter's teeth were being examined by the dentist (who, by the way, was very pleased with her exam), Tony spoke to us candidly about his directorial debut, stereotyping in Hollywood, being Arab American, the importance of family, and his plans for the future.

Directorial Debut

Antoine Faisal and Lynne Vittorio: Let's talk about Made Up. *The trailer looks great.*

Tony Shalhoub: It really is funny. We set out to make a comedy that crosses generations, crosses over from being just a chick flick . . . it's not really what I would describe as a romantic comedy. It's an all around, sophisticated, character-driven comedy.

What type of profile audience are you targeting through Made Up?

We're not targeting any one audience. We want this to be the kind of movie that appeals to a lot of different kinds of people of different ages. It's adult in content but there isn't anything objectionable in it. People can bring their children to it, especially teenagers. Brooke has a teen-aged daughter in the film, played by Eva Amurri, so there's a lot about a mother-daughter relationship. There's a lot of great family stuff that involves sisters—Brooke and her real life sister play sisters in the movie. I think it would have a broad appeal if people gave it a chance.

I understand there have been some problems getting it distributed.

When we first finished the movie, we sent it around to a lot of film festivals where it performed really well and won numerous prizes. We just had a lot of difficulty finding a distributor. I'm not really sure what the reason is. I think distribution companies are less apt to take a chance with something that isn't completely recognizable in form and loaded up with a lot of bankable stars.

What happened with *My Big Fat Greek Wedding*, for example . . . there were all kinds of companies that turned that movie down and did not recognize the potential there and it turned out to make almost 300 million dollars. I'm sure a lot of people lost their jobs over that decision.

We decided to distribute it ourselves. We contacted a number of theaters in New York and here in Los Angeles, to begin with, that are willing to run these movies without a distributor and that's how we're going about it. The Angelika in New York, which is a very high profile theater, really responded to the movie and believes in it.

What was it like working with your wife?

(cautious, mildly maniacal laughter)

Well, it was fantastic. Our whole relationship is based in the workplace. We met doing a play on Broadway, *The Heidi Chronicles*, and we've worked together a number of times since then, both on stage and in television. We always love going back to that.

You've worked together as actors, but this is the first time directing her.

Absolutely. It was, basically, the first time in our long marriage that I was actually able to get her to do what I wanted her to do.

What was it like for you to be behind the camera for the first time?

At first, it was terrifying because it's such a daunting task, but after about a week, I got into it and I fell in love with the whole process. I think I would like to do it again as soon as possible.

You know that way before 9/11, there's been a lot of negative stereotyping of Arabs in Hollywood...

Absolutely.

How have you managed to avoid being stereotyped?

I'm not sure, exactly, how I managed to do that. I was trained in the theater and the emphasis of my training was on playing characters. Transforming, stretching yourself, and trying not to play yourself too much. In the theater, I had a lot of practice doing a lot of different kinds of characters and that translated into my television and film work.

Because of my looks, I was called on to do different kinds of ethnic roles—Hispanic, Greek, Italian, sometimes Middle Eastern, sometimes Jewish, even Russian . . . whatever came along. But I tried to steer clear of those roles that I felt were stereotypical, and not just Arab or Arab American roles, but other kinds of stereotypical roles as well. I was less likely to pursue roles that I felt were stereotypical Italian roles or Hispanic or Mexican or whatever else.

I tried to do that in all of my characters. I tried to bring something new and fresh and unexpected and even when I thought there were aspects in those roles as written that were somewhat stereotypical, I tried to put a different kind of a spin on them.

As far as Middle Eastern roles, I did one television role early on, when I was living in New York and doing mostly theater, and I sort of regretted it and just vowed that I would never do that again.

You know that The Siege[1] *got a lot of flak from the*

1. *The Siege* (1998) is set in New York City. It portrays a terrorist campaign by Arab Americans which the government responds to by rounding up all Arab males and placing them in detention camps. The American-Arab Anti-Discrimination Committee condemned the film for portraying Arabs and Muslims as inherently threatening.

Arab American community. Did you regret playing your role in The Siege?

I don't regret having done that movie. There is a lot that happens in a movie between the time it's written and the time it's shot and the time that it's edited. There were things, when I read the script, I didn't feel that what I read was really what ended up on the screen. There were different aspects of the story that appealed to me. There was an Arab American character that I thought was a positive character, a sympathetic character, realistic but not a goody two shoes, someone who was well rounded.

There were other aspects of the script that I thought were worthwhile and important, like the idea of Arab Americans rounded up and put in interment camps, racial profiling, the danger, in terms of how our government might react to some kind of terrorist activity. Civil liberties and people's freedoms being infringed upon, and basic parts of our Constitution being compromised. Those were the ideas that I thought, when I read the script, were the emphasis of the piece. When a movie is edited and marketed and so forth, different aspects of a movie can be emphasized and I think that's sort of what happened in this case.

A Daring Project

When you decided to make T is for Terrorist,[2] *did you have any concerns about how it would change the way people looked at you in Hollywood? It was a very daring film, very important.*

You mean that I might be stereotyped or somehow profiled in Hollywood?

Yes.

No. It wasn't a concern. I believed in the project and I

---

2. a satirical portrait of the stereotyping of Arabs and Muslims in Hollywood films

believed in the people who made the movie and what they are trying to do as Egyptian Americans. In fact, we're working on another project together—that they're writing and I'm going to help produce and hopefully, be in—that is a very important story about Arab Americans and more along the lines of *Do The Right Thing* or *Barbershop* [films about African Americans]—a real look into the Arab American community.

I think it's an incredibly risky and daring project but that's kind of what I'm interested in right now, alongside the other films I do and the television show, *Monk*. Those are the kinds of things that I'm trying to do because, I've been a director now, I've been a producer on *Monk* for a couple of years and now I realize that I have the ability to begin on this whole other tack in my career. These are the stories I would like to be a part of telling because it's a whole untapped minority group whose voices need to be heard, whether they're comedians or playwrights or screenwriters or directors.

How has the response been to T is for Terrorist?

I have heard that people have liked it and responded to it. I guess if I'm hearing your question correctly, I don't worry about how it will reflect on me or my position in the industry. I feel like I have quite a large body of work now and I'm not really fearful of any kind of backlash.

In Big Night, *you played an Italian chef. Why do you think we haven't seen films like* Big Night, *only about Arab Americans?*

I'm not sure what the reason is. That's exactly what I'm trying to do right now. I'm trying to seek out and support people who are filmmakers and writers who have these stories to tell about Arabs and Arab Americans. I don't know the reason why it hasn't happened yet, but I don't think it's ever too late to start.

Do you see a sitcom portraying the lives of Arab Amer-

icans as being successful in America, especially after 9/11?

I don't see any reason why it shouldn't be successful. I think it would be a really, really tricky thing to pull off but the truth is, if the material is good—authentic, startling, interesting—and the people involved are talented and really doing their work, there's no reason why it shouldn't succeed.

There are very few sitcoms that cover every spectrum. There are certain sitcoms that are geared to certain audiences. I'm not a seer, I don't know how successful or how well embraced a sitcom like that would be, but I certainly wouldn't say it's out of the realm of possibility.

Who are some of the Arab American entertainers with whom you are in contact?

I know Casey Kasem, who isn't an actor, but a personality; Kathy Najimy, I know her, too. There is a whole crop of younger people who are Palestinian, Syrian, Egyptian, Lebanese, who are trying their hand at it. They're not people whose names you would recognize yet. There's a big push out here right now in this community and I'm trying to keep my ear to the ground and give support where I can and relate my own experiences, if that's of any help to anyone.

You were among those in the entertainment industry who came out publicly against the war in Iraq. Have you experienced any backlash as a result of that?

I've known that I have taken certain hits in various conservative newspaper articles and websites and such, but in terms of the entertainment industry, I haven't felt any backlash at all about that. I've spoken my mind, I tried to do my homework and speak intelligently on this subject. I believe that our policy was and is misguided there and I will continue to speak out.

A Lebanese Upbringing

You gave a very moving speech when you accepted your Emmy for your role in Monk. *For many in the Arab Amer-*

*ican community the importance you placed on family res-
onated with their own experiences. How did the values
you were raised with impact your life and would you say
that your upbringing was "Arab American"?*

Both my parents were Lebanese. My father was born
there and my mother's parents were born there. Family
was very important, we had a lot of Arabic food, my parents and grandparents spoke Arabic—at least to each other
when they didn't want us to know what they were talking
about. . . but we were raised in the Midwest, in a middle
class upbringing. We were definitely aware of our roots.
We had a lot of relatives around us. We were also raised
with the idea of inclusion, that everybody should be able
to get along, and even though we didn't want to forget our
heritage, we knew we were in a country that was a melting
pot and that everybody needed to figure out how to oper-
ate together.

But I do think my upbringing has carried over into my
adult life. There has always been a big emphasis on family.
I'm from a family of 10 children and we've all remained
close, even though we all live in different parts of the country, and we get together a couple of times a year. We try to
keep all of the kids, all of the cousins close, so I do think
that is attributed to the way our parents raised us.

*Who are the entertainers that you admired growing
up?*

There are so many. I was a huge admirer of Peter Sell-
ers, Alan Arkin, John Cassavettes, and of course, [the
Egyptian actor] Omar Sharif, because I knew he was sort
of paving the way for me. I still have not met him, but I
hope to. His last name is the same as mine. Hopefully, one
day, we'll work together or at least meet.

What about [Arab American actor] Danny Thomas?

Oh, of course, we watched Danny Thomas. He was very
popular in our house. I was a kid at that time but my par-

ents and my older siblings and all our relatives were kind
of obsessed with that show.

Have you ever been to Lebanon?

No, but I'm planning a trip this year because these
people are interested in me playing Kahlil Gibran.[3] I've
been wanting to go there for years, because my father would
describe what it was like, but I haven't been able to yet.

Are you starting to learn or refresh your Arabic?

Well, I'm going to start. For me to say "refresh" would
be not totally truthful because I knew so little of it growing up, but I would love to begin to pursue that.

(Antoine speaks Arabic).

(Pause . . . then, in a deadpan voice) OK, I'll remember
that.

*I was asking you if I spoke Arabic to you would you
understand what I was saying, but, apparently not.*

Apparently not.

(laughter).

---

3. Kahlil Gibran was a poet and illustrator who emigrated from Lebanon to America in
1895. His most famous book *The Prophet* has been translated into twenty languages.

Ralph Nader

Justin Martin

Consumer activist Ralph Nader was the son of Lebanese immigrants. According to Justin Martin, the author of this selection on Nader's childhood, Nader's parents instilled in their young son a passionate love for the representative democracy of their adopted homeland. In Winsted, Connecticut, Nader had the opportunity to participate in New England town meetings, where he witnessed democracy at work on a local level. In 1965, after attending Princeton and Harvard Law School, Nader wrote the book that first made him famous, *Unsafe at Any Speed: The Designed-In Dangers of the American Automobile.* In it he charged that the American automobile industry put profits above driver safety in their design of automobiles. As a result of this groundbreaking work, Congress enacted a series of safety measures, including mandating the installation of seat belts in all U.S. cars. Nader went on to launch the consumer movement when he founded Public Citizen in 1971, which continues to fight for the rights of ordinary citizens against huge corporations and big government. In 2000 Nader became the first Arab American to run for president, running on the Green Party ticket against Republican George W. Bush and Democrat Al Gore. Ultimately, Bush prevailed.

Ralph Nader was born during a blizzard on February 27, 1934. His three older siblings had been delivered at home and this time his mother was intent on giving birth at the hospital. The hospital, she figured, would give her a chance to rest. But the snow made it impossible and thus Ralph

Justin Martin, *Nader: Crusader, Spoiler, Icon.* New York: Basic Books, 2002. Copyright © 2002 by Justin Martin. Reproduced by permission of Basic Books, a member of Perseus Books, LLC.

also was born at home. Shafeek was then eight years old, and the only Nader child with an Arabic name. Sisters Claire and Laura were five and two.

His Parents Emigrate from Lebanon

Nathra Nader—Ralph's father—had come to the United States from Lebanon in 1912. At the time, he had $20 and a sixth-grade education, and knew nary a word of English. He worked a series of jobs—at the Maxwell Auto Works in Detroit, a machine shop in Newark, a shoe factory in Lawrence, Massachusetts—until he saved up enough money to be a proper provider. Then he returned to Lebanon briefly to find a bride.

Rose Bouziane—Ralph's mother—was part of a sprawling family of eight daughters, two nephews, and two nieces raised under a single sod roof in Zahle, Lebanon. The family farmed and tended sheep. It was an arranged marriage, but Nathra and Rose were well suited. Nathra was an extreme personality: obstreperous, deeply moved by perceived injustice, and given to bursts of untamed idealism. He was tall and lean with something of the ascetic about him, as if all that restless mental energy were burning off calories. Like Nathra, Rose had had a variety of experiences by a very young age: she had grown up in a Christian family surrounded by Muslims in Lebanon under the French mandate.[1] She was a natural teacher. When she and Nathra met, she was teaching French and Arabic. She was small and striking, with coal-black eyes and light, light skin. It is from Rose that Ralph and his siblings got their complexion, and their practical sense.

Rose married Nathra in 1925 and returned with him to America. The couple lived in Danbury for a year before moving to the town of Winsted, Connecticut. . . .

1. Lebanon was part of the Ottoman Empire until the empire crumbled at the end of World War I. Between 1919 and 1947 it was governed by France under the mandate system.

Upon moving to Winsted, Nathra opened the Highland Sweet Shop, a bakery that over the years would expand into a full restaurant. The Naders also bought a house on a hill near downtown. It had two stories and ten rooms, and was built in 1917; there the four Nader children were born, quite literally, and raised.

Even as a small child, Ralph was astonishingly precocious. For example, his three older siblings might be learning a song in Arabic. Little Ralph was simply present in the room. Suddenly he would announce that he knew the song, and, to prove the point, he would then sing it from beginning to end. No one even expected him to pay attention, let alone learn the song faster than his brother and sisters. . . .

A Year of Nader's Childhood Spent in Lebanon

When Ralph was three, he went to Lebanon for a year. The trip was the fulfillment of a promise Nathra had made to Rose's family: During the first fifteen years of marriage she would return at least once to Zahle for a visit. Nathra remained behind in Winsted. . . .

In Zahle, Lebanon, the Nader children enjoyed being surrounded by Rose's hyperextended family. Besides Rose's seven sisters, two nephews, and two nieces, there were scores of cousins of varying ages. One cousin—certain that the visitors missed American-style Christmas—looked up Santa Claus in an encyclopedia and did her best to dress the part. An aunt who knew English taught the older Nader children so they would not fall behind in their schooling. They picked figs in the Bouzaine family orchard and took long walks in the lush Bekaa Valley.

A high point of the trip was a visit to Arsoun, the tiny village where Nathra had grown up. The kids got a thrill out of the bullet holes in the ceiling of Nathra's boyhood home. The holes were the remnants of a Lebanese wedding custom. When Nathra and Rose were married, well-wishers fired off a salute as they entered the house. . . .

During the year in Lebanon, an archbishop called on the Bouziane household. He wanted to meet the visitors from America and offer them blessings. One by one, various relatives went up and kissed the archbishop's ring. When it was Ralph's turn he refused, saying: "I don't have to kiss your ring. I'm an American."

Everyone laughed. The archbishop tousled Ralph's hair.

"Who knows what led a four-year-old boy to do that?" recalls Nader. "It wasn't anything about the archbishop. It was more that I didn't want to defer like that. I probably would have agreed to sit in his lap and let him tell me a story. But there was something about the ring."

American Democracy at Work

Upon returning from Lebanon, the family was confronted with the question of whether Ralph was ready to start elementary school. He spoke English but had also picked up a fair amount of Arabic, and he mixed the two languages with abandon. Rose descended on the staff of the grade school near the Nader home, insisting that Ralph be allowed to attend. In 1939 he began going to the Fourth School, a classic brick schoolhouse nicknamed "Big Red.". . .

From an early age, he received a double dose of civics. He got it at home from his parents, who were sober—to the point of high earnestness—about the values of America. Equality, representative democracy, freedom of expression: these were not simply pieties to be tossed about by vote-hungry politicians. These were the promises of the Naders' adopted land. "When I passed the Statue of Liberty I took it seriously," Nathra was fond of saying. He was forever on the lookout for fresh examples of democracy in action and was shocked anew each time he detected hypocrisy or injustice. Ralph got a second jolt of civics from the town of Winsted itself. Many immigrant families settle in large cities, but long before Ralph was born, Nathra had his fill of Newarks and Detroits. He and Rose decided to raise a family in small-town New England.

Young Ralph's world was characterized by a remarkable degree of immediateness and accessibility. Sometimes lying in bed at night he could hear the cows mooing in the fields just outside of town. When he awoke in the morning, there would be fresh milk, delivered in glass bottles. All of Winsted's institutions—civic and otherwise—were within easy walking distance. "The library was right around the corner," he recalls. "The schools, the post office, the city hall, the town center—everything was within fifteen minutes."

When Ralph was about eight, Nathra began taking him to the county courthouse to watch lawyers argue cases. Under his father's tutelage, Ralph came to view penny-ante property disputes and the like as epic battles between the strong and weak, rich and poor, just and unjust. Early on, he vowed that he would also be a lawyer when he grew up, and not just any lawyer: he would represent underdogs, in keeping with the most sacred principles of democracy.

At a tender age, Ralph was introduced to town meetings, New England–style. This is a peculiar and regionally specific form of governance, developed by colonial-era settlers itching to escape the tight grip of the British monarchy. Long after the American Revolution, certainly well into the twentieth century, town meetings remained a vital democratic institution in New England. As of the 1930s, Winsted had a mayor and a board of selectmen. But their decisions had to meet with the approval of the townspeople. According to Winsted's charter, as amended in 1915, a quorum of just 10 percent of residents was required to alter ordinances, shoot down a statute, and so forth.

All of Winsted would show up for the meetings. This

was bare-fisted democracy; often people got into heated personal arguments or were hooted into submission. "Value that person," Nathra would say to his children, whenever someone took a particularly unpopular stand. Certainly Nathra was not afraid to go it alone. He waged a long and solitary battle to improve Winsted's sewers. As the Nader children got older, they were also urged to add their voices to the clamor at the ever fractious Winsted town meetings.

CHRONOLOGY

1854
The first known Arab immigrant, Antonios Bishallany, arrives in America and settles in Boston.

1876
Arabs exhibiting their wares at the Centennial Exhibition in Philadelphia return home with favorable views about America.

1880s
In this decade an estimated twenty-five hundred Arab immigrants arrive in America. Many become peddlers, a trade that takes them traveling throughout the country.

1892
America's first newspaper in Arabic, *Kawkab Amerika* (*Star of America*), is published.

1890–1895
Arab Christians establish Melchite, Maronite, and Syrian Orthodox churches in New York City.

1907
A court case establishes that Syrians are not Asians and therefore are not subject to the exclusionary laws that deny Asian immigrants citizenship at this time.

1916
The Ford Motor Company employs over five hundred men in Detroit, mainly Syrians who are joined by increasing numbers of Iraqi Chaldeans.

1917

The Syrian Ladies' Aid Society is founded in Boston to help Arabs in the homelands during World War I. Its affiliates later offer services and support to Arab American immigrant women.

1918

Over thirteen thousand Arab Americans serve in World War I.

1923

Kahlil Gibran publishes *The Prophet*, one of America's best-selling books of all time. The first mosque is consecrated in Highland Park, Michigan.

1924

The first wave of Arab immigration to America comes to a close with the restrictive Immigration Act of 1924. By this date approximately 124,000 Arabs have settled in America. Ninety percent of first-wave immigrants are Christian.

1936

The Arab League in America is established to support Palestinians in their fight against the British and the Zionists who want to establish a homeland for Jews in Palestine.

1948

An Arab-Israeli war creates 750,000 Palestinian refugees. Most flee to neighboring Arab countries, but increasing numbers arrive in the United States.

1950s

Arab American actor Danny Thomas stars in one of America's favorite television shows, *Make Room for Daddy*.

1952

The Federation of Islamic Associations is founded to unify Muslim communities in the United States.

1965

The Immigration and Nationality Act of 1965 reopens America's doors to worldwide immigration; this initiates a second wave of Arab immigration, which is 60 percent Muslim. Arab American Ralph Nader publishes *Unsafe at Any Speed*, a book that revolutionizes the car industry and launches the consumer advocate movement in America.

1967

The Six-Day War is fought between Israel and a coalition of Arab countries after which Israel occupies the Palestinian territories; this initiates a new influx of Palestinian refugees to America. The Arab-American University Graduates (AAUG) is founded to give voice to the Arab perspective on the Arab-Israeli conflict.

1968–1970

Over thirty-seven thousand Arab professionals immigrate to the United States. Included are many Palestinian refugees and Egyptians disillusioned with economic reforms under President Gamal Nasser.

1972

James Abourezk of South Dakota becomes the first Arab American senator.

1975

Civil war erupts in Lebanon, initiating a new influx of Lebanese to America. The Arab Community Center for Economic and Social Services is founded in Dearborn, Michigan.

1976

Mary Rose Oakar of Cleveland, Ohio, becomes the first Arab American congresswoman.

1978

Palestinian-born professor Edward Said of Columbia University publishes *Orientalism*, a book that exposes underlying prejudices in Western scholarship about the Middle East.

1980s

The decade witnesses a wave of terrorism in many places around the world, prompting President Ronald Reagan to begin a "War on International Terrorism." Arab Americans in the United States experience a wave of hate crimes as Americans vent their fears and frustrations on them.

1980

The American-Arab Anti-Discrimination Committee (ADC) is founded by former senator James Abourezk to counter stereotypes about Arab Americans and to fight discrimination.

1985

The Arab American Institute (AAI) organizes to help Arab Americans get elected to public office.

1986

Congress opens hearings on anti-Arab hate crimes.

1988

Senator George Mitchell, an Arab American from Maine, becomes U.S. Senate majority leader.

1990

Arab American professor Elias Corey of Harvard University wins the Nobel Prize in chemistry.

1991

A wave of Iraqi immigration to America follows the Persian Gulf War. Between 1991 and 2003 approximately fifty thousand Iraqis settle in the United States.

1993–2000

President Bill Clinton appoints Arab American Donna

Shalala secretary of health and human resources. She serves in the cabinet for two terms.

1999

Arab American professor Ahmed Zewail of the California Institute of Technology wins the Nobel Prize in chemistry.

2001

The terrorist attacks of September 11 lead to a new wave of hate crimes committed against Arab Americans.

2003

Many Arab American organizations join the American Civil Liberties Union in filing a legal challenge to section 215 of the U.S. PATRIOT Act, which Congress passed in 2001 as a means to fight terrorism; it grants the government expanded powers to secretly obtain the personal records of citizens. Arab American organizations estimate that 3 million Americans trace their roots to an Arab country.

FOR FURTHER RESEARCH

Past and Present History

Nabeel Abraham and Andrew Shryock, eds., *Arab Detroit: From Margin to Mainstream*. Detroit: Wayne State University Press, 2000.

Sameer Y. Abraham and Nabeel Abraham, eds., *Arabs in the New World: Studies on Arab-American Communities*. Detroit: Wayne State University Press, 1983.

Baha Abu-Laban and Michael W. Suleiman, eds., *Arab Americans: Continuity and Change*. Belmont, MA: Association of Arab-American University Graduates, 1989.

Anan Ameri and Dawn Ramey, eds., *Arab American Encyclopedia*. Detroit: U-X-L, 2000.

Barbara C. Aswad, ed., *Arabic Speaking Communities in American Cities*. New York: Center for Migration Studies of New York and the Association of Arab-American University Graduates, 1974.

Kathleen Benson and Philip M. Kayal, eds., *A Community of Many Worlds: Arab Americans in New York City*. New York: Museum of the City of New York/Syracuse University Press, 2002.

Larry Ekin and Leila Gorchev, eds., *1991 Report on Anti-Arab Hate Crimes: Political and Hate Violence Against Arab-Americans*. Washington, DC: American-Arab Anti-Discrimination Committee, 1992.

Abdo A. Elkholy, *The Arab Moslems in the United States: Religion and Assimilation*. New Haven, CT: College & University Press, 1966.

John L. Esposito and Yvonne Yazbeck Haddad, eds., *Muslims on the Americanization Path?* Atlanta: Scholars, 1998.

Eric J. Hooglund, ed., *Crossing the Waters: Arabic-Speaking Immigrants to the United States Before 1940.* Washington, DC: Smithsonian Institution Press, 1987.

———, ed., *Taking Root: Arab-American Community Studies.* Vol. 2. Washington, DC: American-Arab Anti-Discrimination Committee, 1985.

Albert Hourani, *A History of the Arab Peoples.* New York: Warner, 1991.

Hussein Ibish, ed., *1998–2000 Report on Hate Crimes and Discrimination Against Arab Americans.* Washington, DC: American-Arab Anti-Discrimination Committee, 2001.

———, ed., *Report on Hate Crimes and Discrimination Against Arab Americans: The Post–September 11 Backlash, September 11, 2001–October 11, 2002.* Washington, DC: American-Arab Anti-Discrimination Committee, 2003.

Philip M. Kayal and Joseph M. Kayal, *The Syrian-Lebanese in America: A Study in Religion and Assimilation.* New York: Twayne, 1975.

Michael S. Lee, *Healing the Nation: The Arab American Experience After September 11.* Washington, DC: Arab American Institute, 2002.

Ernest McCarus, ed., *The Development of Arab-American Identity.* Ann Arbor: University of Michigan Press, 1994.

Alixa Naff, *Becoming American: The Early Arab Immigrant Experience.* Carbondale: Southern Illinois University Press, 1985.

Gregory Orfalea, *Before the Flames: A Quest for the History of Arab Americans.* Austin: University of Texas Press, 1988.

Don Peretz, *The Middle East Today.* Westport, CT: Praeger, 1994.

Yossi Shain, *Arab-Americans in the 1990s: What Next for the Diaspora?* Tel Aviv: Tel Aviv University, 1996.

Evelyn Shakir, *Bint Arab: Arab and Arab American Women in the United States.* Westport, CT: Praeger, 1997.

Michael W. Suleiman, ed., *Arabs in America: Building a New Future.* Philadelphia: Temple University Press, 1999.

Adele L. Younis, *The Coming of the Arabic-Speaking People to the United States.* Ed. Philip M. Kayal. Staten Island, NY: Center for Migration Studies, 1995.

James Zogby, ed. *Taking Root Bearing Fruit: The Arab-American Experience.* Washington, DC: American-Arab Anti-Discrimination Committee, 1984.

Biography and Memoir

James G. Abourezk, *Advise & Dissent: Memoirs of South Dakota and the U.S. Senate.* Chicago: Lawrence Hill, 1989.

Leila Ahmed, *A Border Passage: From Cairo to America—A Woman's Journey.* New York: Penguin, 1999.

Munir Akash and Khaled Mattawa, *Post-Gibran Anthology of New Arab American Writing.* Syracuse, NY: Syracuse University Press, 1999.

Jean Gibran and Khalil Gibran, *Khalil Gibran: His Life and World.* New York: Interlink, 1996.

Naomi Shihab Nye, *Never in a Hurry: Essays on People and Places.* Columbia: University of South Carolina Press, 1996.

Salom Rizk, *Syrian Yankee.* New York: Doubleday, 1943.

Edward Said, *The Edward Said Reader.* Eds. Moustafa Bayoumi and Andrew Rubin. New York: Vintage, 2000.

————, *Out of Place: A Memoir.* New York: Vintage, 1999.

Web Sites

American-Arab Anti-Discrimination Committee, www.adc. org. This site offers up-to-date information about the Arab American community and its efforts to combat discrimination.

Arab-American Business, 2000–2002, www.arabamerican business.com. A magazine with back issues online featuring news about Arab American entrepreneurs.

Arab American Institute, www.aaiusa.org. This Web site offers a wealth of information about Arab Americans, polls of Arab American opinion on a variety of issues, and position papers on recent issues.

Café Arabica, The Arab American Online Community Center, www.cafearabica.com/nuke. A compendium of reprinted articles about the Arab American community and an online discussion board.

Council on Islamic Education, www.cie.org. Materials about the teaching of Islam, including guides to Islamic holidays.

Detroit Free Press, www.freep.com/jobspage/arabs. Current and back issues of a newspaper that covers many topics of interest to Arab Americans in the Detroit area, the site of America's largest Arab American community.

Washington Report, www.washington-report.org/back issues. Published by the American Educational Trust, this Web site publishes articles from the magazine *Washington Report* pertaining to U.S. relations with the Middle East.

INDEX